FLYING ALONE

a memoir

FLYING ALONE

a memoir

BETH RUGGIERO YORK

For Daddy,
Who has always been with me, even when I thought I was alone

THE PROMISE

The TWA Boeing 707 accelerated for takeoff and forced me back into my seat. The thrill and excitement were tangible, the first I'd felt since my father's death earlier that year. At fourteen years old and traveling alone for the first time, my mother was sending me for a summer visit with relatives in Colorado. At that moment, I made a binding promise to myself that someday I would learn to fly.

CHAPTER 1

Starting Out

I cranked the starter on the fuel truck a second time, and it started with a painful groan. This early in the morning, I was the first person on the east side of the airport, except for the controller working in the tower overhead. Rod, my boss, had left early the day before, in the rain, so I made the rounds this morning fueling the airplanes I hadn't filled the day before. Either I got busy taking care of the airplanes on the ramp, or I would be the victim of Rod's morning mood until whiskey time started.

I was working from the ground up to reach my goal of flying for the airlines—taking flying lessons and working the line at New England Flyers, a tiny fight school in Beverly, Massachusetts. I had begun lessons for the private pilot license in the dead of winter. It was the first rung of the ladder to a job with the airlines, but there were many more rungs above that. The FAA required ground school and a minimum of forty hours of flight time before taking the private pilot ground and flight tests, but it would probably take fifty or sixty hours, maybe more. From there, there was the instrument rating, the multi-engine rating, the commercial license, multiple flight instructor ratings...and then the Airline Transport Pilot license.

And experience, lots and lots of experience in the form of flying hours. The magic number was around three thousand before a major airline would even look at me.

It was a long road ahead, but I was up for the task, ready to prove myself in a man's world, ready to make my father proud. I imagined him watching me from above, just as he had so many years ago. I was six years old, standing on a sidewalk next to Lawrence Hospital with my mother and brother. As I looked up to the fourth-floor window, Daddy looked down. He waved and smiled. I waved back. I didn't know why he was in the hospital, and my mother only told me he did not feel well. Children could not visit patients, so I had to wave from below. I didn't question it, but my six-year-old mind still wondered what could be wrong.

When he came home a week later, everything seemed to be back to normal. My parents never talked about it, but I never forgot.

Then, when I was thirteen, my father suddenly returned to the hospital. It was November 1975. I still didn't know why, just that he was sick and would be home soon. I didn't make the connection with the first hospitalization seven years earlier, but my now thirteen-year-old mind questioned what was happening. He came home for Thanksgiving but returned to the hospital the next day. Two days later, my mother came into my room at bedtime. She sat on the edge of my bed and told me I could not go on the school ski trip. The trip was going to be the highlight of my eighth-grade school year, so it disappointed me in a typical adolescent way. When I asked why, she said, "In case something happens." I saw then that my father would never come home.

He didn't come home for Christmas the next month. One month later, on January 24, 1976, Mom came into my room in the early morning and again sat on the edge of my bed. She told me Daddy had died during the night. I later learned he had leukemia. They diagnosed it when we visited him at the hospital seven years earlier. The doctors had given him five to ten years to live.

My father died, and everything changed for our family in that moment. The loss would affect each of us profoundly. For me, an adolescent girl just coming of age, what should have been a gradual change from childhood to maturity was instead abrupt. It marked the end of my sheltered life. He wouldn't be there to guide me on the road to becoming a confident young woman. I missed him desperately and communicated with him in a diary of nightly letters to him about my days. Glancing back, the void in my life was the need for male approval. I began to look for that from boyfriends but never found what I subconsciously needed. He'd been gone a long time now, but I hoped he was proud. Maybe he wasn't proud of the fueling part—not after my college education—but perhaps he was proud of the flying part. I would prove myself in this man's world of aviation, both to my father and for myself.

I pulled out from the usual parking spot in front of the jet-fuel pump and swung the heavy old truck around to the line of flight school airplanes. These were the most important aircraft to keep filled with the fuel I hauled. The six airplanes that comprised Rod's existence needed to be ready to fly at any time. All were leased back to the school by individual owners, all except one—N8655F—November-Eight-Six-Five-Five-Foxtrot, or Five-Five-Fox for short. Rod owned that one. It had new paint, got the most baths, and was always the first to fly.

On Rod's line of airplanes, only Five-Five-Fox needed fuel this morning. I positioned the truck in front of the propeller, jumped down from the cab, and pulled the heavy fuel hose from its reel over to the right wing. It was a Piper Cherokee 140—PA 28-140—one of the most common civil aviation training aircraft models in flight schools across the country with 150 horsepower. Its competition included the Cessna 152 and 172 models, both high-wing aircraft.

These Cherokees were older airplanes, mostly 1960s vintage, and if you couldn't tell their age from the outside because they'd had new paint, then you could almost always tell on the inside with one look at the instrument panel. Five-Five-Fox was like that. She had shiny red and blue stripes on a white background. Inside, though, the instrument panel and radios were dated and incomplete. It had the basics for communication with air traffic control but none of the more sophisticated equipment that would allow instrument flying in the clouds. This airplane was only qualified to fly in clear weather.

Hershey Bar–shaped wings distinguished the Cherokee 140s. My flight instructor, Steve Puchalski, told me early on that these planes were good for training because the stable wing shape made it impossible to hurt yourself.

"You forgot the ground wire." Steve's voice startled me as he came from behind the truck. I had replaced him as Rod's lineman, so he trained me how to operate the fuel truck, just as he was my teaching me how to fly an airplane. He was the newest and most ambitious instructor at the school. "Check the oil in Ninety-Zulu, it's down a quart and a half. I'm taking it out in twenty minutes with a student."

"I'll get it in a second. Let me finish this one," I said. I didn't tell him I had not bothered to check the oil in Ninety-Zulu this morning, or in any of the planes for that matter. After all, he had been the one who told me not to bother checking the oil every time.

"Forget it. I'll get it." He walked to the back of the truck and opened the compartment where Rod stored the oil and funnel. "There's only one quart in here."

"Damn," I mumbled under my breath. "Okay, I'll go get it now."

I ran inside for the key to the shed, ran back to the shed, and hauled out a case of oil. Steve stood by Ninety-Zulu while I struggled up the ramp's incline to the truck. *No help with this one*, I thought. *Better get used to it.* Seven thirty in the morning, and I had already broken a sweat. I handed him the second quart.

He propped up the engine cowling and unscrewed the oil cap. The cowling came down with a bang on his hand, and he swore. He struggled with the funnel, cowling, and oil, finally holding the cowling with one hand and dropping the funnel on the ground so he could pour the oil directly into the opening. I bent down and picked up the funnel as it rolled down the ramp.

"You know, this is a new funnel. It'll stay in the inlet by itself. You don't have to hold it," I said, offering it back to him.

"Whatever," Steve mumbled. He didn't smile. It seemed he rarely did, and the way he looked at me with his dark eyes always made me nervous.

Steve poured the first quart and handed me the empty container. I leaned back against the wing and waited until he finished with the second. He wore his usual pair of jeans and a T-shirt. Today he wore a New England Flyers T-shirt—red, white, and blue. The clothes revealed his lanky build, usually hidden under a leather flight jacket for most of the winter months I had known him. He was not tall, just a few inches taller than my sixty-four inches. As he poured the oil, I noticed that his shoulders had a permanent stoop. It was part of what defined his personality, but I still had not come up with what that definition was. As hard as I tried to know him, he remained aloof and unreachable. He maneuvered himself with skill, much the same as the skill he used taking the airplanes into the air and back down again.

"When do we fly next?" he asked in his flight instructor voice. "We have to start the prep work for your flight test." I was almost ready for my private pilot check ride.

"Tomorrow afternoon," I answered. "Rod said I could have the time off to fly every other day until I'm ready for the test. And plenty of time on weekends. Adam will fill in for me."

Adam Kraft was a part-time lineman who filled in the extra hours fueling airplanes and doing other odd jobs for Rod. He was not too far out of high school and already had his private license. The hours working the line earned him the extra money he needed to continue his training. Like me, he spent his days at the airport, flying, working, or hanging around watching other people fly. And drinking Rod's booze. Seagrams V.O., Rod's whiskey of choice, was the one thing Rod was not stingy with. "If ya ain't flyin'," he'd say, "help yourself to a nip or two. But only after the flyin's done for the day. Break that rule and it won't just be me comin' after ya, there'll be the Feds, too."

For Adam and me, it was that nip or two in the late afternoon or evening that we looked forward to after a long day hauling fuel hoses, scrubbing airplane bellies, and being yelled for by airplane owners and corporate pilots with their cool sunglasses and gold-trimmed Learjets. And, of course, Rod.

With the cowling closed and two empty bottles in my hands, Steve continued the pre-flight check. "When you take your flight test," he said, "remember the unspoken rule—Rod expects the large bottle of V.O. along with his fee of a hundred dollars, cash money." Rod was also the FAA flight examiner on the field.

"But he sends me to buy a liter bottle for him almost every day!"

"Yeah, but he has to pay for that." He laid a hand on my shoulder. "This way, he gets free booze." Steve finally smiled. "And we get to drink it, too. We'll celebrate with it when you pass your test." He winked.

Beverly Airport, East Side
New England Flyers was the yellow building to the right of the control tower

—

We were all employed by Rodney Gorham, owner of New England Flyers, veteran flyer, and World War II veteran. He had blue, crescent-shaped eyes, the eyes of an old man. The scrutinizing look often revealed a poor mood, at least until time to open his bottle of V.O., an afternoon ritual at the flight school.

Then his eyes showed the glint of a smile. When he finally did smile around two or three o'clock, I couldn't decide if it was for love of his little flight school as he watched the planes come and go on the ramp outside the window, or if it was just a pure Canadian whiskey smile as he anticipated another night with his girlfriend. I was never sure.

Rod indeed had the weathered look of the old pilot that he was. He rarely mentioned his past, but conversations with some of the airport regulars—aka airport bums—revealed that Rod had been a bomber pilot in the Royal Canadian Air Force during World War II. He was shot down over Germany and became a prisoner of war.

Day after day, he sat on a stool behind the dirty counter in the flight school looking out on the ramp, with a soggy cigar hanging between his lips. The planes came and went, and Rod made a mental note of each. If I missed refueling one, he would yell out, "You gotta fill Five-Five-Fox! It's goin' out again in five minutes!"

By the end of the day, he stunk with the stogies and the whiskey, but he was happy, and before he took off, leaving New England Flyers in the hands of the employees and the airport bums, Rod made a trip to the bathroom and came out with a clean shave and the smell of cheap cologne. It didn't take long to know that on those nights, Rod was either with his girlfriend or at the dog races at Wonderland Greyhound Park in Revere.

Everyone at the airport who knew Rod knew of his comings and goings, and everyone at Beverly airport knew him. He had been there with his school a lot of years, the whole operation transported to Beverly Airport in an old school bus back in the 1950s when the old Revere Airport became a shopping center. Rod was a local legend, disliked by some but loved by most.

The sound of a rough engine took our attention, and we turned to see Rod driving down the ramp between the lines of airplanes. Today he was driving the "shitbox," as everyone called his old maroon Chrysler. Most days, he drove the airport rental car, but when it was rented, he took the shitbox. And that often meant a sour mood, so I climbed into the truck to continue my rounds, and Steve headed back across the ramp to the office.

Rod had a scowl on his face as he went into the office with Steve right behind him. Without a doubt, though, Steve was his favorite instructor, mostly because he followed along in Rod's old-school "seat of your pants" approach to flying. Even so, Rod ran the school in keeping with the Federal Aviation Administration regulations that had emerged and evolved since his days flying a bomber over Europe. He was an FAA-designated examiner for flight tests of all types, but he was also in the business to make a living. It served him well to have an active knowledge of the regulations, so he instinctively knew when to follow them and how to bend them ever so slightly to keep his planes flying and generating income.

I pulled the truck up to the first airplane on the keep-full list. These were the airplanes in the flight school along with the privately owned ones on the ramp that always needed the fuel topped off in preparation for flight. This one was a Cessna 182 Skylane, a high-wing, single-engine airplane, more powerful than Rod's low-wing Cherokees. I looked for the chalk mark on the Cessna's nosewheel. That was my signal that the plane had or had not moved since last being fueled. I didn't see a chalk mark on this one, yet I knew it hardly ever flew. Recalling the previous night's rain, it occurred to me that the chalk marks would have washed away. I groaned. I would have to check each one.

I hauled the ladder to the left wing of the Skylane and climbed up to unscrew the fuel cap. Full. Climb down and carry the ladder to the right wing. Also full. I packed up the ladder and drove the truck to the next one on the line. Another Cessna. Up on the ladder. Full. I sighed loudly. The next one had been flown, so I pulled the hose from the reel on the fuel truck, hauling it out with all my weight and the nozzle slung over my shoulder. Lifting it up the ladder, I leaned against the wing and boosted it up to the inlet on top of the wing. I had already broken a sweat.

My mind drifted from the smell of aviation fuel and the hum of the fuel pump, things that had become so familiar after only a few weeks on the job. My path to the airlines could have been much easier. The original plan was to get the best flight training available by joining the Navy, but it had fallen apart just a few weeks before. I had passed all the tests and was ready to sign on when my recruiter, Karen, drove me to the Naval Air Station in Newport, Rhode Island for the last hurdle—a medical exam. There was a glitch in my history, and I prayed it would not be a problem.

As I sat in a chair, the Navy doctor looked deep into my eyes with a light.

"Look left," he instructed.

I looked left.

"Look right."

I looked right.

"Now look straight ahead."

When he finished, he said, "I don't see scarring or damage to your left eye." My hopes were momentarily high, until he continued, "But you're too much of a liability."

My heart bottomed out. Just what I was afraid of. A year earlier, shortly after graduating college with a degree in Chinese Studies and near fluency in Mandarin Chinese, I'd gotten a job leading tour groups to China. At the start of my first tour, I developed the worst headache I'd ever had. It was painful to move my left eye in any direction. I tried to ignore it, but a few days later, the vision became blurry and kept getting worse. After a week, I left the group one afternoon to visit the local hospital. They showed me into a dingy examination room.

The Chinese doctor held a light in front of my left eye while I stared at his nose. "I need to do a test," he said, turning the light off. He told me what the test was and what he was testing for, but my Chinese did not include medical terminology, so I didn't know what he was saying, except that he suspected meningitis. I understood that because he used the English word.

He gave instructions to the nurse standing behind him. While he assembled syringes and other unidentified tools, she led me to the other side of the room and instructed me to lie on the examination table covered with a not-so-white sheet. The doctor came over carrying a syringe with a very long needle, rolled me onto my side and slowly pushed the needle into my lower back. The pain was intense. I felt woozy and passed out. I later learned that he had done a spinal tap, another new word for me in both Chinese and English.

When we got to Beijing, I proceeded to the US Embassy and to see the resident American doctor. He also looked into my eyes for several minutes with a light. When he was done, he told me he didn't know what it was, but I needed to return to the US right away. After more tests in the US, including my second spinal tap in a week, they told me it was optic neuritis, which I later learned was a classic first presentation of a disease called multiple sclerosis. They officially diagnosed me with "probable MS." It wasn't MS until it happened more than once—hence *multiple* sclerosis.

It was treated successfully and hadn't recurred. The Navy doctor said my eye showed no scarring, but even "probable MS" ruled out a career in military aviation.

And that was it. Joining the Navy was not to be. It was a big setback, but I recovered by devising a new course through the world of flying. I resolved to continue climbing my way to the airlines on the civilian path. It would still get me there, and it would still make my father proud.

Three more rows of airplanes, eight per row, needed to be checked along with the ones behind the maintenance hangar. When I finished with that, I had to scrub the bellies of Rod's own airplanes. I swung the truck around, fighting as always with the manual steering, and began the next row with another Cessna.

These were my first impressions of the world of aviation: Rod, bottles of Canadian whiskey, working the line...and my flight instructor, Steve. I had started as the official lineperson at New England Flyers on April 27, 1985, my twenty-third birthday, four months into flight lessons with Steve for my private license. Aviation had already swallowed me whole.

CHAPTER 2

Becoming Involved

"Congratulations," Steve leaned over and whispered in my ear. He turned my face to his and kissed me with unexpected passion. The sexual tension had been high all night as I celebrated my new license.

"First step to the airlines," I whispered back, excitement in my voice. More kissing.

"You have Rod's official FAA blessing...you're a private pilot now."

We were leaning against the pool table in the flight school basement. Our faces were close, lips touching, and the couple of shots of whiskey I'd had courtesy of Rod after I passed the flight test made the scene dreamlike. My flight instructor had made the move I'd been hoping for.

CHAPTER 3

Rolling

The following days were exciting and still dreamlike as I tried to make sense of it all. My flight instructor was now my boyfriend. Steve was two years younger than me, but he seemed to know it all, and I was determined to learn it all from him. His control over the airplane was complete and never in doubt. Even when he yelled from the right seat of the airplane if I didn't show that same control. "Don't let the airplane fly you. You fly the airplane!" He said it as if the airplane was a living thing, an animal or a child that needed discipline and absolute control. At those times, I couldn't help feeling I was the airplane, and Steve was flying me.

I had more licenses and ratings to get through with him. But not only was I his student and now his girlfriend, I was also the lineman—or rather, lineperson—fueling the airplanes and doing all the other grunt jobs a lineperson does, like scrubbing airplane bellies and cleaning the toilets in the flight school.

Five-Five-Fox taxied onto the ramp with Tim Knight's early morning solo student. I drove the truck to the bottom of the ramp and swung it around, ready to fill the airplane as soon as they tied it down. It was one of Rod's rules that the truck never be put in reverse, and he made sure no one ever forgot, along with the story of how that rule came about. Something about a previous lineman backing the truck into one of Rod's planes. Not someone else's plane, Rod's plane. I quickly made it a standard operating procedure to plan my driving path well in advance so there would never be a need to put the truck in reverse. With two walls of large windows for Rod to oversee all activity on the ramp, he could monitor my movements, even though the windows were thickly coated with cigar smoke. I made sure backing up the truck would never be an issue.

The sun was already getting warm as I pulled out the fuel hose from the side of the truck. There would be no escaping today's heat and humidity during this unseasonable hot spell. Rod did not allow us to use the old air conditioner built into the office wall. In fact, it was so old and rusty that I wondered if it even worked. With no breeze these past few days, the black tarmac would radiate heat all day until it was unbearable.

I looked across the grass behind the airplane to watch a small corporate jet landing on Runway 34. Rod would tune in to Unicom[1] right about now hoping the jet would taxi to his side of the field to buy fuel. I held my breath and waited, letting it out slowly as the airplane turned left at the end of the runway and taxied to the west side of the airport. Fueling jets was my most dreaded job as the lineperson. I felt intimidated standing on the ramp to guide them to within inches of the jet fuel pump (the truck did not carry jet fuel), using hand signals I didn't really know. Often, I made sure I was out of sight when a jet taxied

---

1   UNICOM (universal communications) is a radio frequency at each airport for planes to communicate with the service providers on an airfield to arrange fuel or parking. At uncontrolled airports, UNICOM is also used for incoming and outgoing planes to announce their location and which runway they'll be landing on.

onto the ramp, arriving only after they had parked themselves beside the pump. Let them be responsible for scraping a wing tip. There were already enough headaches with this job.

Even if I avoided parking them, though, I equally dreaded the fueling process. I needed more body weight, and often the jet pilots—young and middle-aged men, cocky with the knowledge they had just arrived in the heaviest iron on the field—would get a good chuckle as they watched me drag the fuel hose like a pony in a pull contest. Between the heat and the heavy hose, it was an exhausting process. From what I was learning about multiple sclerosis, heat sensitivity and fatigue were big symptoms. I couldn't help but wonder if my exhaustion was because of that. It made a difficult job even more difficult.

"Pretty good view from behind in those jeans," Steve said. "We're flying tonight, right?"

I tried not to smile but did kind of like the compliment. "Seven o'clock in Five-Two-Five," I answered.

Seven-Two-Five-Two-Five was one of Rod's Piper Warriors, a step up from a Cherokee 140 in horsepower, weight, equipment and age. Piper had exchanged the Hershey bar–shaped wing of the Cherokee 140 and some of Piper's other older models for a tapered wing design on the Warrior, and that changed some flight characteristics. Because these aircraft were newer and had better avionics, they were the only ones on Rod's line certified for IFR—instrument flight rules for flying in the clouds. The Cherokee 140s did not have the instruments required for IFR, so graduating to the Warriors meant a lot at New England Flyers. Now that I was working on my instrument rating, we were flying the Warriors only. It was more expensive to rent them, but there was no choice. For my private license training, the Cherokees were forty dollars an hour wet—that meant fuel was included in the price. The Warriors were fifty dollars an hour wet.

"I figure that will give us an hour or so before it gets dark, unless you want to do some nighttime instrument work," I said.

"No, we'll just do airwork. I'll show you some things I couldn't show you before you got your private." Steve's eyes sparked with a hint of something I hadn't seen before as he turned back to the office.

"Teach me or show me," I called after him.

"Some things you just have to learn yourself," he responded without turning around.

Rod stepped out of the building and yelled, "Hey, Puchalski! Get in here! Your student's waiting." Steve didn't change his pace.

Rod was in a pretty good mood today. Usually when he went home to his wife the night before—that meant no booze, no girlfriend and, I guessed, no sex—his mood was a lot better than if he had a hangover and a tired body to nurse the next day. I turned my attention back to the fuel hose.

———

Five-Two-Five was another leaseback on Rod's line. A wealthy Saudi man owned it, and he only flew it when he wanted to impress a date. It had the basic equipment needed for instrument flight and not much more. The transponder worked, so the controllers could always see where we were. That was of primary importance. There were dual radios and dual VOR[2]

_____

2   VOR (Very High Frequency Omnidirectional Range Station) is a common type of radio navigational aid. The white transmitters on the ground can be recognized by their huge cone shape, often on or near airports.

receivers for navigation, and what they called an Automatic Direction Finder for doing practice instrument approaches. Instrument flying was about using the instruments and radios to get to the right place at the right time. When I passed the test, it would add the rating to my private license, and I could fly in the clouds legally.

Steve sent me out to do the pre-flight inspection while he ate a ham and cheese sub at Rod's desk. I'd picked it up for him when I made the afternoon liquor-store run for Rod. The store was out of Rod's favorite cigars, but there was plenty of whiskey, and he was now on his way to a smile.

"You mind if I fly left seat tonight?" Steve asked as he approached the plane. "Sometimes I think I've forgotten how. Besides, you need to start learning to fly from the right seat when it's time for your instructor ratings."

My instructor ratings were a long way off, and at this point in my aviation career—and it had become a career—it didn't seem I would ever get to that level. My private license was only four days old, and I had a grand total of only sixty-two flight hours. I was counting on Steve to guide me further down the road. He led, and I followed.

"You said you wanted to show me a few things anyway," I answered and stood aside as he climbed in first. The only entry door was on the right side, so the left-seat pilot needed to climb in first.

I latched my seatbelt but left the door open for air. "You can do the checklist since you're in the left seat," I said, holding out the clipboard for him. He took it and promptly stuffed it in the door pocket.

"If you really want to be a pilot, then you learn to fly without a checklist. Just keep it all up here for the day you need it." He pointed to his head. "Most of the time, it's all so routine you don't even have to think about it."

Wow! This was a different Steve. I was shocked but tried not to show it. Was this the way it really was? I came from a very rules-based background—there were rules, and I followed them. Now, my flight instructor was giving me a new "rule" that was entirely contrary to what I previously understood. In my new world of aviation, though, Steve was the king of flying, and his rules were the rules. Still, I wondered if this was how every pilot did it or if he was just such a skilled pilot that he could get away with it.

"It's not how you would have learned it in the Navy. This is real-world flying," he said with a touch of arrogance.

He ran his fingers across the circuit breaker panel to feel for any that had popped, and then over to the switches. He turned on the master switch and fuel pump. Five-Two-Five was humming the familiar sounds now. He opened the tiny pilot's window and yelled, not too clearly, "Clear!" The prop was turning before anyone would have had the chance to run clear. It caught on the first spin, the engine was running, and the microphone was in Steve's hand. "Ground control, Seven-Two-Five-Two-Five, east ramp, ready to taxi with information Charlie."

"Charlie" was the code word for the current airport conditions recorded on the Automatic Terminal Information Service (ATIS). It told us the wind direction and speed, barometer setting, visibility, and runway in use, along with other pertinent details. The ATIS information was pre-recorded by the tower controllers and could be heard on its own radio frequency. As the conditions and details changed, the tower controllers changed the recording and the code word, which progressed through the phonetic alphabet. This evening, the weather was stable, so when we returned from our flight, the information would likely only have changed to Delta, if it changed at all.

"Roger, Five-Two-Five, taxi to Runway 34," the female voice came back. The tower was directly behind us, and all the voices were familiar. This was Laverne, whose voice maintained a monotone at all times.

I looked at him, surprised by how fast he went through the procedures. I almost couldn't keep up with him. "How did you know the information was Charlie?"

"I got it on the radio in the office before I came out." Steve released the brake and punched the throttle up to get out of the parking spot. "Ground, Five-Two-Five requesting an intersection takeoff."

"Roger, Five-Two-Five, taxi to Runway 34 at the intersection."

Steve flipped the frequency to control tower, where the controllers who handled takeoff and landing spend their days. "Tower, Five-Two-Five ready for takeoff. Right turn out."

"Five-two-five, cleared for takeoff at the intersection." It was still Laverne. Apparently, she was alone in the tower tonight manning both ground and tower functions.

The words were barely out of her mouth, and Steve had Five-Two-Five rolling onto the runway and right into the take-off, popping down two notches of flaps as we hit the runway centerline. With a takeoff at the intersection, roughly one third beyond the start of the runway and flaps down, he was showing off his short-field takeoff technique. The flaps on takeoff added lift to the wings so we would be off the ground more quickly. Left hand on the yoke, right on the throttle, he pulled the plane into the air at precisely the moment it could fly and held it a few feet above the runway in what was called ground effect, making it feel like we were floating as we continued to accelerate to gain enough speed for the climb. If only I could have shown such an efficient short field technique when we were preparing for my flight test. But that took practice in real-life situations, and Steve promised I would get plenty of that.

With the flaps back up to zero degrees, he climbed at just above the stall speed[3] to get the maximum climb angle. Now and then, he pushed the nose down to check for traffic. He was quiet as we flew to the northeast from the airport. We passed over Hamilton and Ipswich and then on toward Plum Island and the ocean. This was what we called the 'practice area,' uncontrolled airspace with very little traffic, where we could safely practice flight maneuvers. It had become familiar terrain to me during my private license training, and I recognized every feature on the ground between Beverly and the practice area. This time, though, I watched Steve's own movements rather than the visual references outside the plane. It was the first time I had been in a plane with Steve flying from the left seat, and I couldn't help but feel in awe of his confident movements.

His flying style was distinctive, just like most everything else about him. It all just carried over into the airplane, the car, and the bedroom. Nothing was tentative or appeared unplanned. Control was unmistakable.

We climbed to three thousand feet, the standard altitude for airwork practice, and leveled. He pulled the power back to 2,300 RPM, leaned the fuel mixture, and trimmed the aircraft for virtually hands-off flight. The air was clear and still, a beautiful evening for flying. We flew up the coast from Plum Island,

---

3   Stall is a dangerous situation when an aircraft drops dramatically because of a too-low airspeed and/or too-high angle of attack (nose pointing up).

and I waited for his next move. Eventually, Steve turned east over the water.

"You want to see a roll in one of these things?" he asked.

"You can't roll a Warrior," I said in disbelief. Rod and Steve always told me that the Piper low-wing aircraft could do nothing aerobatic. Not even a spin unless you tried really hard, and even then, it was never a full spin.

"You can do anything you want with it—you just have to know the airplane well enough. Watch this."

He pulled back the power and edged the nose down to gain speed. I tried to make mental note of his moves, but in the next moment, I lost all ability to keep track of them as the plane reached some unknown speed in a nose-down attitude, and Steve yanked on the yoke and turned it hard. The right wing dropped violently. I felt the effects of aileron and rudder action as the blood in my head moved with the roll like a momentary high.

And then it was over. Steve's hands and feet seemed to have hardly moved, and we leveled at just two hundred feet below the starting altitude.

"Wow!" I laughed out loud. "That was wild!"

Steve had a self-satisfied grin on his face.

"It was over so fast, though. How about once more so I can see how you did it?" I was not scared. No; instead I was in even more awe of his flying skills, and as my admiration grew, so did my own goals. I trusted him.

"Okay. This time to the left," he agreed. He was definitely enjoying it.

Once again, nose down, speed up, nose back up, power, left wing down...and we rolled to the left with aileron and rudder forces I still did not understand. Steve leveled the wings, facing the ocean. This time I just smiled. Rolling was sexy, flying was sexy, and Steve was sexy.

The sun cast a reddish-orange glow as it set behind us, reflecting in the water below. Such a peaceful night, and he was twisting it all around with these maneuvers. No other boyfriend I'd had thrilled me like Steve. My boyfriends from high school and college were boring in comparison. I was smarter than them and achieved more than they did. Steve, though, was on a whole different playing field.

"So are you going to tell me how to do it?" I looked at him, waiting for enlightenment.

"It's just a matter of gathering enough speed by stuffing the nose down and then forcing it into the roll with enough aileron and opposite rudder. You've got to be real sure with all the moves, especially in this airplane, because you don't want to lose it halfway and fall through when you're inverted. If you think about the effects of the controls you're using, it makes perfect sense."

Well, maybe it made sense to him. It was still a jumble of different manipulations in my mind, though I memorized what he said—"speed, aileron, and opposite rudder"—and tucked it away for future reference with all the other things he was teaching me.

He turned the airplane back toward Beverly and switched the radio to the ATIS frequency, 118.7, to hear Laverne's recorded voice still sounding very bored, now with information Delta.

"What are you doing tonight?" he asked.

"Nothing."

"How about Bloody Marys at my house?"

"Sounds good." Excitement over anything except aviation would never show in Steve's words, so I found it necessary to keep my own enthusiasm contained. He was cool, and I needed to keep cool.

"You like Bloody Marys, don't you? With horseradish and hot sauce, real hot?"

I nodded. It wouldn't have mattered what drink or how spicy it was.

"Five-Two-Five cleared to land," Laverne said as we turned from base leg to final leg in the landing pattern.

"Roger, Five-Two-Five," he confirmed in his radio voice. "Good. We'll pick up the stuff on the way home. My brother might be home, but my father's up at the house in Maine."

"He has a house in Maine?"

The wheels rolled onto the runway in a perfect full stall landing.

"Five-Two-Five, taxi back to the ramp."

"Roger, Five-Two-Five, taxi to the ramp," came the tower response.

"It's just an old house my father bought a long time ago. Kind of a shithole really. Needs a lot of work and has no running water or electricity. But we still like it, and the area is pretty. You'll have to come up sometime."

I hung on those last words. His father's "shithole" could have been in Newark, and they would have had the same impact. "I was thinking of having the whole airport crew up there for a long weekend or something," he continued. "Maybe you could come up then. You know, like Rod does every year for Labor Day weekend."

I was immediately deflated. "The whole airport crew"? Is that how he felt about me? Was I just one of the proverbial gang?

"No, I don't know," I said, less interested now and even a little annoyed. "What does Rod do?"

He pulled in front of the tie-down spot and shut the engine down. "He has everyone—New England Flyers including the airport bums, his family, friends, students, everyone and anyone—up to his camp in Vermont. We roast a whole pig and camp there for the night. It's a real good time."

He tied the wings down while I tied the tail, and we walked back to the office. The lights were on inside, and I could see the usual gathering through the large windows. I cringed when one face came into view. It was Harriet. She was always there. Her frequent, apparently purposeless appearances at New England Flyers always lasted for hours.

Even though she had her private license from years before, Harriet never flew, at least not that I had ever seen. From all observations, I could class Harriet with the airport bums—the old farts, as Rod called them—non-active pilots who never flew anymore but spent endless hours in Rod's little waiting area, smoking, drinking whiskey, and telling stories of their flying days. Some had been airline captains, flight engineers, or navigators, but some were amateurs who spent their retirement building experimental aircraft kits at home in the garage. Except for Harriet. She did nothing.

Harriet was in her mid-thirties, a large woman with prematurely gray hair. Her entire social life seemed to be the New England Flyers waiting area, perpetually in waiting while others her age came and went, learning to fly and getting jobs. Not Harriet. She just hung around listening to everyone else's stories. She usually arrived about five thirty in the afternoon when she got off work. I think she sold insurance.

Steve, however, had been another part of her social life in the months before my arrival at the flight school. While I was working on my private, Steve occasionally came to work in the same clothes two days in a row. This happened a few times before I put it together with corroborating comments each of them made. I couldn't understand it. She was unattractive and twelve years older than Steve. At least I was just two years older. Maybe he ended up with her because the pickings for girlfriends in aviation were slim and she was better than nothing. I really couldn't imagine why, and it drove me crazy. Some airport bums called her Harry, for short, because of her masculine appearance. Harriet backed off when Steve and I started dating, but her time at the airport did not change, and it made me uncomfortable.

"Hi, guys," came Steve's usual greeting as we walked in the door.

There were five in the room, including Harriet, each with a paper cup filled with Rod's booze. Jerry Kennedy, one of the younger airport bums who did fly, sat with the bottle between his legs.

"Rod's gone home, Steve," Harriet told him as she reached for the bottle between Jerry's legs. "He said you have to fly early tomorrow, so check the schedule."

I rolled my eyes. She even acted like his mother.

"Shoot some pool, Steve?" Norm Guidaboni asked him. Norm was a retired Eastern Airlines captain.

"No, not tonight, Norm. I'm going to head home if I have to fly early," Steve answered. "Anyway, you beat me the last two times. I can't afford three times in the same week." The pool table was in the basement along with the ground-school classroom. It was an alternate spot some nights after the flying was done.

We left New England Flyers in their care. They were often the ones who locked up after they had drunk Rod's bottle dry. The next day I would have to replace it with my usual trip to the store for whiskey and stogies.

We drove separately to Steve's house, stopping on the way for Bloody Mary supplies and a few snacks. When we got there, the house was dark, so I figured his father and brother were not home. We unloaded the bags, and Steve began mixing the drinks.

Life for these three men in the Puchalski home was strange, at best. Only occasionally did I see his father or brother. If they weren't out, then they were likely behind the closed doors of their respective bedrooms. The origins of Steve's nature were not hard to imagine. His father was a coarse man with a bitter attitude toward life, and his brother disliked his father, spending most of his time alone in his bedroom. Mrs. Puchalski, Steve's mother, had died many years before. Steve's only spoken memory of her was of a sweet woman who hated her husband and loved her sons. He told me many times that his parents did not speak to each other for years before she developed cancer, after which they still did not speak. She died when Steve was twelve years old, leaving him only with the memory of a woman who hated her husband.

The family lived in the same house as they did when she was alive. The small living room was never used, nor was Mrs. Puchalski's bedroom. She'd had her own. These rooms, never touched since her death, seemed to be shrines to her memory even though that memory was bittersweet for all in the house.

On the fireplace were pictures of her with her husband in his uniform from the war, and later with her sons. She had a warm face and smile, and Steve looked like her, though his own face had taken on much of his father's cynicism. I occasionally wandered into the living room, looking at those pictures while waiting for Steve, feeling as though I knew her and was sympathetic to her position in the strange, cold house. Whatever chance she had in life to make her sons something of herself was lost when she died. Both Steve and his brother were so much like their father now.

CHAPTER 4

The Cub

We watched from the ramp as the little yellow airplane floated like a leaf down to the runway for landing. The fat, wide wings made for a slow, stable approach speed, much slower even than the Cherokee following behind it, which was forced to do S-turns for spacing. As if unaware of anyone behind or anyone at all, the yellow airplane continued her ever slow, floating approach until it ended in a soft touchdown on the pavement, using just a tiny piece of the runway before turning off. The Cub had arrived.

Beverly was a modern airport with modern aircraft, paved runways, and a control tower. The Cub was a 1946 Piper J-3 and came from another era. It brought nostalgia for the old-timers, and excitement for a few others—those of us at New England Flyers who owned a piece of her. Rod had bought the Cub from a pal of his in New Hampshire, and before she arrived at Beverly, Rod offered her for sale in ten shares, his own eleventh share an honorary one. Eleven hundred dollars bought a membership in the Cub Club and the right to fly the Cub as far as your licenses and ratings allowed.

Steve was the first to buy a share of the Cub. I followed and took the second, knowing it would give me more time flying time and more time with Steve. He was as excited about it as anything I'd seen him get excited about, so it had to be right. The remaining shares were purchased over the next few weeks—some airport bums who rarely flew, some private pilots who wanted to own a piece of a vintage plane for little money. A little extra money paid for insurance and a maintenance kitty. When it quickly became clear Steve and I would do most of the Cub's flying, I knew it was a good choice.

This Cub had a power upgrade from its original Lycoming sixty-five-horsepower engine to a one-hundred-horsepower Continental engine. This was a huge boost. It also came with a pair of pontoons for water landings and a pair of skis for landing on snow in the winter. What it lacked was an electrical system, though, which meant it had no starter and no radio. It had to be hand-propped to start, just as in the old days. Our radio was a handheld, battery-powered unit that Rod bought from an aviation mail-order catalog.

The Cub's call sign was N4434T, Three-Four-Tango for short, but to everyone on the field, including the controllers in the tower, she was The Cub, the only Cub on the field, and also one of only a handful of vintage taildraggers—aircraft that use a tailwheel and two forward wheels rather than tricycle-style landing gear like the Cherokees—at Beverly.

By Wednesday, Rod had Steve checked out in the airplane after only two hours of time in the air together. Steve's three-point landings, all wheels touching down at the same time, were nauseatingly flawless from the start and, after Rod sent him to fly it solo, Steve then taught himself the wheel landing—the two front wheels rolling onto the runway first at a little higher approach speed before the tailwheel touched.

Rod explained these landings to us repeatedly in the office during the weeks before and after its arrival as if it was the closest reality would get him to the early days of his flight school after the war had ended. His explanations were filled with wistful remembrances of the past, usually after he'd taken the whiskey level in the bottle down a few inches. But in between the reminiscences of an old man was the unquestionable understanding that only came with years of experience and twelve thousand hours of flying time.

If we were doing our tricycle gear landings in the Cherokees, he told us, the way we were taught—full stall as we hit the runway, yoke all the way back—then the three-point landing would be a cinch. But, Rod said, the two-point wheel landings were like cheating. Just fly the airplane onto the runway before the tail touches down, give the stick a little flick of the wrist forward to hold her on the mains. Keep that tail off until it was ready to touch down, nice and easy. Rod used his hand to demonstrate that flick of the wrist, the crux of the wheel landing's success. All I could picture, though, was the simple little flick being a big flick, and instead of the tail dropping down nice and easy, the Cub's nose hitting the ground and destroying the propeller.

Rod had a strong warning for us, though, and that was to fly her onto the runway straight, especially in a crosswind, or she'd make you pay with what he called a ground loop, and that could be disastrous. Or at least very embarrassing. And it was in just those adverse conditions of strong crosswinds or gusty winds that the wheel landing was needed because it allowed you to bring the plane in faster and therefore with more control.

A couple of weeks later, on a Friday morning, Rod checked me out for solo flight in the Cub. It had taken Steve just a short familiarization with the airplane before he caught on to flying her with finesse and confidence. For me, I reflected with frustration, it took over two weeks and a total of ten hours. Sure,

Steve had over one thousand hours of flight time, and I had only 120, but I still had trouble accepting that perfection had not yet arrived at my door. So, when the day came that I could fly the Cub by myself, I vowed to give myself vigorous self-training workouts of landings, loops, and spins. It was my effort to inch closer to Steve's level in the airplane.

I scheduled my workouts to start promptly at six in the morning, just after the sun rose over the left wing of the Cub in her tie-down spot. For the third time that first week, I arrived at the field early, first one there, only one there, no one even in the tower, and pre-flighted and prepared her for flight. I stood in front of the nose and rubbed my hands together to prepare for the task of starting her. I was still new at this business of hand propping an airplane, but even when Steve was there, I would never give in to asking for his help. My arms were strong enough, even after a half dozen tries to start her with no results, and I would show that I could handle all that he could.

I planted my feet firmly on the grass in front of the propeller, right foot forward and wide of the left foot. Rocking back and forth a couple of times to check my stability, I brought both hands up to the blade already positioned for the engine's power stroke. *One, two*…on three I put all my weight into my arms and threw the prop. The engine sputtered, turned a couple times, and then died quickly. Again, *one, two, three*…I threw the prop again, and this time the engine turned over.

Propping an airplane without someone inside at the controls was not an acceptable practice in general aviation, but because the Cub idled at a very low RPM with the throttle all the way back, Rod decreed that it was safe for us to hand-prop alone without someone inside holding the brakes, instead with the tail and wings still tied down. This was especially fortunate because the brakes never worked too well. The Cub's tie-down spot was behind Rod's row of Cherokees on a slight uphill incline on the grass, all the better to help keep her in place after the prop was spinning and before the pilot climbed in.

By the time I had untied the tail and wings, kicked the chocks out from the tires, and climbed in, I was already tired. I taxied to the runway, shaking my head disgustedly. I was too young to feel this way. Was this part of multiple sclerosis?

I brought my attention back to the immediate task and announced I would be taking off on the quiet frequency. I advanced the throttle. Before it even reached three-quarters of its travel, and the airplane had only rolled two hundred feet down the mile-long runway, I was airborne, climbing like a kite, pushing higher and higher. The morning air was still cool, and I rose easily to 3,400 feet. There were still a few hours before the July humidity would take hold. It was the only time of day when the outline of the coast and the horizon would be so crisp. I flew over the beaches of Manchester and Magnolia, and out to Cape Ann. I followed the railroad tracks and then descended to fly low over the inlets with the window open. This little airplane would add hours to my logbook, taking me a step closer to the airlines. It was an exhilarating time to enjoy flying and to forget about the fuel truck and Thursday's bounced landing.

CHAPTER 5

Instruments

The cloudy, rainy days outnumbered the clear days that summer, so when we couldn't fly the Cub, I continued to work on my instrument training with Steve to take advantage of the low ceilings and poor visibility. There had been only a few days when we could not sneak out because the ceiling was too low. Profits at the flight school were scant on rainy days, and this summer had shown Rod plenty of that. The airplanes weren't flying, and the fuel wasn't flowing. Rod would rather take me off the clock and send me up flying with Steve for a couple hours of revenue while he handled any fueling himself. So that is what he did.

Steve's enthusiasm for these flying conditions was contagious, and I quickly learned to love the challenge and thrill of instrument flying. "Being in the soup is the best kind of experience," he told me. And the lower the overcast, the lower the visibility, the more we did. I was well on my way to the important instrument rating, one step closer to the commercial license, followed by the instructor ratings. And then I would have all that Steve had. From there it was just a matter of logging flight hours.

On the way to the airport, I tried to guess the ceiling of the early-morning clouds. Two hundred feet, five hundred feet, one thousand feet…and the visibility—a quarter mile, a half mile, a mile. The buildings weren't tall enough to help make a good estimate on the ceiling, not unless it was overcast at one hundred or two hundred feet. But Route 114 took me from Marblehead to Salem and then over the bridge where, depending on the visibility, I would have a good view of the stacks at the Salem power plant. With their tops at five hundred feet, they were the best gauge. When I arrived at the airport, ATIS would tell me how close my guess was, and with each week of predominantly poor weather, my guesses were becoming more accurate.

Steve had shown me the back way to the airport over the Kernwood Bridge instead of the Beverly Bridge. It brought me through less of Salem and more of Beverly each morning, avoiding traffic. It also went by his own neighborhood in Salem where he lived with his father and brother.

This morning and every morning, a tight feeling knotted my chest as I approached the street that led to Steve's house, wondering if he was there. On days when we had not been together the night before, I sometimes risked a drive by his house to check for his ugly green car, an American Motors Pacer. If it wasn't there, my predetermined conclusion would be that he had spent the night with Harriet as he had been known to do in the past before me. I tried to fight the thought, but it was always there, just as Steve's car was always there, and I would then scold myself for having doubts, which stemmed from my lack of confidence.

I resisted the urge to drive by his house this morning, and it took until Kernwood Bridge to lose the tightness that gripped me.

When I unlocked the flight school door, the smell of whiskey and stale smoke hit me in the face. As usual, the airport bums had not cleaned up the night before. I walked over to the radio on the counter and turned it on, listening carefully.

*BEVERLY AIRPORT INFORMATION BRAVO.
1200 ZULU[4] WEATHER. ESTIMATED CEILING
SEVEN HUNDRED OVERCAST, VISIBILITY ONE
HALF MILE IN RAIN AND FOG. TEMPERATURE
SIX SEVEN. DEW POINT SIX FOUR. WIND ONE
FIVE ZERO AT EIGHT KNOTS. ALTIMETER
TWO NINER EIGHT NINER. APPROACH IN USE
LOCALIZER ONE SIX, LANDING RUNWAY ONE
SIX. ADVISE YOU HAVE BRAVO.*

Close enough. I had guessed six hundred feet and a half mile visibility. Their "estimated ceiling seven hundred overcast" was as much a guess as mine unless they had an actual pilot report from an arriving or departing aircraft.

We needed a six-hundred-foot ceiling to file a flight plan for an instrument training flight. That was Rod's rule to ensure we could return with his airplane. Beverly's most sophisticated instrument approach only allowed descent to 580 feet before a pilot was required to declare a missed approach and either go-around for another try or go to another airport. If we could find our way to the runway, then we could legally depart, no matter what the conditions. But we might not get back in.

---

4   The term 'Zulu' refers to Greenwich Mean Time. The FAA uses GMT for all operations. In this case, 0045 Zulu was 7:45 p.m. (five hours added to Eastern Standard Time).

"What's the ceiling?" Steve asked as he breezed through the door. He was in early this morning. I looked at him, hoping as always for a positive indication that there was more between us at this point than ceilings and approaches.

...INFORMATION BRAVO. 1200 ZULU WEATHER. ESTIMATED CEILING SEVEN HUNDRED OVERCAST, VISIBILITY ONE-HALF MILE IN RAIN AND FOG. TEMPERATURE...

ATIS told him before I could. I switched the radio off.

He enjoyed hearing that. "Good. Did you file a flight plan yet?"

"Not yet. I want to wait for Rod so there's someone here to fuel."

Steve came behind the counter and picked up the phone, squeezing me as he did, followed by a brief kiss. In fact, it was so brief and so non-committal that my stomach clenched for the second time this morning. This feeling usually came as I spent futile moments waiting for more from him, more commitment, more that showed he was into me as much as I was into him.

He dialed the number for the Flight Service Station.

———

"Four thousand feet, direct to Manchester as filed" were the instructions. I took Five-Two-Five up to altitude and turned on course toward Manchester Airport in New Hampshire. Steve shuffled through the approach charts on his lap and did not pay attention to this segment of the flight. Flying the route was the easy part of instrument flight—climbing to altitude, then straight and level between navigational aids with occasional radio communication. He could trust me with this. By now, I was proficient.

One, two, three approach charts—he arranged them and clipped them to my kneeboard. The ILS[5] for Runway 35, VOR approach for Runway 35, and the most dreaded non-directional beacon (aka NDB) approach to Runway 35, all instrument approach choices for Beverly Airport. I hated NDB approaches because they were the most imprecise, only leaving you in the general vicinity of the runway.

Steve took the radio and requested multiple practice approaches into Manchester Airport, and the session began. I went to work juggling altitude, course, radio communications, and timing. Steve watched the instruments calmly, with occasional comments. *Watch your heading. What altitude are you supposed to be at right now? When are you planning to begin your descent? Did you start your timing? Are you going to tell the tower you're on the missed approach?*

The way he asked these questions made me feel stupid, and I sometimes answered with a quick "Sorry." He rarely raised his voice, but I always knew when he was annoyed with a less than perfect performance. He was probably no different when he was teaching his other students, except now the frustration was closer and more personal for me since we were going out. There was now a gray area, and I took any annoyance he showed as personal disapproval that carried over into our relationship.

---

5   Instrument Landing System: This is a precision instrument runway approach that gives descent and runway alignment guidance. At that time, it was the approach that allowed the airplane to descend as low as two hundred feet above the ground with minimum visibility.

Still, he taught, and I tried to learn. I wanted to learn everything he knew. I wanted to fly the airplane, not let the airplane fly me, but it seemed the more I learned, the greater his own skill, and the further he was from me. I flew every day that I could, and when I wasn't flying, I studied, listened, read, and watched. But the hours were too few to catch up to him. Of course, I could never catch up. He had ten times more hours than I had, but I thought that if I were more advanced and had more hours, maybe I would have more confidence in the relationship. I was caught in a self-defeating cycle of my own making. Steve was flying a Learjet while I flew Five-Two-Five.

After a long sequence of approaches, some less humbling than others, we turned back to Beverly in the rain. The clouds were as thick now as when we took off, and the ceiling at Manchester was up and down between six hundred and eight hundred feet. ATIS information Juliet estimated Beverly's ceiling at four hundred feet, the lowest I had yet encountered.

"We can't get in," I said.

"Never say never. You don't just turn around because the idiots in the tower are telling you the ceiling's too low," Steve rebutted. "This is what you call a *real* approach."

He was turning the pages to the well-marked and well-used Beverly approach chart for the localizer to Runway 16. This kind of instrument approach was one step below the precision ILS approach. Where the ILS provided an approach path for exact alignment *and* glide slope of an aircraft to the runway, the localizer only gave approach path alignment and stepped the aircraft down to the minimum altitude in several increments. On an ILS approach, the minimum allowed altitude might be as low as two hundred feet above ground level. Not so with the localizer. At Beverly, we only had to 580 feet before the pilot had to declare the missed approach.

"Here." He shoved the approach chart over and picked up the mike. "I'll handle the radios." I'd seen Steve excited in the airplane like this only a few times before, and it was always when there was a challenge at hand. He cleared the charts we wouldn't be using to prepare for the "real" approach.

"Warrior Five-Two-Five, confirm you have information Juliet," the controller said.

"Roger, Boston, we have Juliet," Steve confirmed.

"Five-Two-Five, turn left heading one four zero until intercept, descend to two thousand feet. Cleared for the localizer to Runway 16 Beverly."

I turned to the assigned heading and began the descent from three thousand feet. Steve had already tuned the radio to the localizer frequency, and I waited for the needle on the instrument panel to come alive to show we were approaching the final course. For my first "real" approach, I was remarkably calm. Steve had told me once I would never know a pilot's tension while he was in the airplane because deep down, I always knew if there was any trouble, it was 'his airplane' and he would fix the problem. Sure, I thought, you're the instructor. And he was right. He was pilot in command. That was why I could do this approach just as though it was for practice, and when we arrived at the designated altitude, I would call the tower to declare a missed approach and climb back up for another. Not for Steve. He knew we had to get in or figure out an alternate plan. That was his responsibility as pilot in command, not mine. At least not yet mine. For now, he held my life in his hands, just as when he showed me how you could roll one of these airplanes.

The needle came alive just as I leveled at two thousand feet. I turned to the localizer heading of 157 degrees and pinned the needle right in the middle where it needed to be, allowing myself a little satisfaction with the accurate turn on course, that is until Steve demanded, "Get down to eighteen hundred feet! They cleared you for the approach! Always keep ahead of the airplane, or you'll screw up every approach you do."

Quickly deflated, I pulled the throttle back enough for the quick two-hundred-foot descent.

"Five-Two-Five, contact Beverly Tower at 125.2. Good day." Boston Approach handed us off.

While Steve was busy with the radio, I tried to get ahead of the airplane. Speed back to ninety knots, level at eighteen hundred feet until final approach, my watch ready to start the timing...

"Beverly Tower, Five-Two-Five with you on the localizer," Steve reported.

"Roger, Five-Two-Five. Report the TAITS marker. Wind is one seven zero at five knots. Last pilot report on the ceiling was two hours ago. They called it at exactly 580 feet. Since then, a Gulfstream and a Lear missed the approach and went on to their alternates."

TAITS was the name of the final approach fix. From there, I would begin our final descent, timing, and speed control while maintaining the localizer course. Fortunately, the wind today was calm, making things easier to manage. The needle for TAITS came alive and moved to the center as we crossed over it. We were a little less than six miles from the runway threshold.

"Five-Two-Five at TAITS," Steve informed the tower.

"Roger, Five-Two-Five, cleared to land. Wind is one seven zero at six knots."

We were now on final approach, the most critical part. I pulled back the throttle and began the descent, balancing it with a constant speed of ninety knots. The designated time at that speed was three minutes and twenty seconds, at which point the missed approach had to be declared if the runway was not in sight because of the clouds.

Sixteen hundred feet. Fourteen hundred. Twelve hundred. I looked at my watch. Two minutes ten seconds left. I kept the descent between four hundred and six hundred feet per minute and adjusted for speed. The rain had stopped, but the clouds were still thick with moisture. This was a solid cloud cover. No breaks at all.

At one thousand feet, I cut the throttle back a little more to quicken the descent. Steve had relinquished the charts to the back seat and was busy looking for breaks in the clouds below us, all the time glancing back at the instruments. He said nothing. Nine hundred feet. Eight hundred feet. We were still in the clouds.

Steve put his hands on the controls. "I've got it now. You do the looking." He adjusted the power. "What's the time?"

"One minute and five seconds to go," I responded.

Passing six hundred feet, we should have leveled at the prescribed five hundred eighty feet until our three minutes and twenty seconds was up. But Steve continued to let the airplane down gradually, one hand on the throttle, one hand on the yoke, still checking outside for any visual references. The cloud cover was not letting up. I opened my mouth to warn him as we passed through five hundred eighty feet but stopped when I looked at him, seeing he was fully aware. The concentration in his face and hands was intense as five hundred feet went by with still no breaks. I thought maybe here he would shove the throttle forward and head out on the missed approach, but he continued.

"Time's up," I announced. He did not respond as he mentally registered the data and gave the instruments a revised scan. Once again, I thought that was what he was waiting for. Instead, we moved through four hundred and forty feet, four hundred and twenty, four hundred. The clouds still did not let up. If the timing and speed had gone as planned, we would have been eight tenths of a mile from the runway threshold after the three minutes and twenty seconds. We were at four hundred feet and probably on a short final leg.

I did not bother with the timing anymore, instead switching back and forth between the clouds outside and the altimeter inside. My participation at this point seemed of little help and even unnecessary as Steve's dominance over the situation was complete.

We passed through three hundred feet.

"There's the white house on a quarter-mile final!" he practically yelled, tipping the right wing down to show me through a small hole in the clouds.

I caught a short glimpse before we went back into the soup again. At 260 feet, I saw small patches of the ground below us. I wondered where the runway sat as we traveled through this mess. The localizer needle showed we were straight on for it, but the breaks we had were not nearly enough to identify the runway and make a landing. Steve continued the descent with the same defiance he showed each time he didn't use the checklist or when he was pushing the airplanes beyond their structural limits. Through 250 feet, it still looked the same—a little better, but not enough. My heart pounded as I wondered how he would end this effort. As far as I could tell, there were two choices, in a tree or on the runway. Still, his confidence in this and all challenges excited me.

Steve pulled more power off as if expecting to land. "I've come this far, I'm not giving it up now," he mumbled. And then, as if the sky was spitting us at the airport, we popped out of the clouds at less than two hundred feet and fully two-thirds of the way down Runway 16. He pulled off the power, added flaps, and yanked the plane into a right turn. Sailing down the runway too fast and too high for a landing, he banked steeply, moving through 110 degrees of turn to align with Runway 27. Full flaps, throttle all the way back, Five-Two-Five had already eaten half the length of the new runway choice. By the time we glided over three quarters of the five-thousand-foot runway, Steve squeaked it on. He brought it to an abrupt stop before turning the 180 degrees to taxi back to the ramp. It had been a strange thrill as he showed me, himself, and even the airplane that he was in charge.

He was smiling with self-satisfaction. "Five-Two-Five, taxi back to the ramp."

"Roger," the voice in the tower replied, "taxi to the ramp." There was a pause, and then the voice asked carefully, "Do you have a pilot report on the ceiling?"

"Six hundred feet," came his quick answer. I raised my eyebrows and looked at him. Steve glanced back at me as we taxied and held his left hand up from the throttle for me to see. It was trembling. He replaced it on the throttle, and we taxied back in silence. I had no words as I tried to digest what he had done. By the time we were at the ramp, Steve was no longer shaking.

"Remember," Steve said carefully, "no matter who asks you, the ceiling was at six hundred feet. It's all part of being a pilot." I nodded.

CHAPTER 6

Formation Flight

I stood in front of the fourth window in the flight school and opened a second roll of paper towels. The insides of the windows were so coated with cigar smoke that the paper came up brown even with the third and fourth wipe. It was a miserable job as the summer sun beat through the glass, but better this than lying on my back scrubbing airplane bellies.

I kept at it while Rod sat behind the counter smoking a big Cuban cigar one of Tim's students gave him, smiling now that he'd had a few nips.

"Ya comin' up tomorrow, ain't ya?" he mumbled with the cigar hanging out of the side of his mouth.

"Of course," I answered.

He already knew the answer, but the Labor Day party at his camp was so important to him, and he wanted to be sure we would all be there.

"You'll fly up in Eighty-Delta and take a couple others with ya. I got Steve in the Cessna. I'd have you two take the Cub up, but you'd spend the whole damn day gettin' there." His eyes sparkled in typical whiskey fashion. Rod was genuinely likable at this time of the day. The sun was shining, and four of his airplanes were flying. With the right combination of circumstances, Rod was undoubtedly likable, even lovable.

I wiped the sweat off my face with a clean towel and stepped back to see the difference in the windows. "I don't know how you ever could see out these windows, Rod. When were they cleaned last?"

He thought about it. "Oh, I'd say Leo Swain musta been the last one to have at 'em. Six, seven years ago."

"Leo Swain?!" I exclaimed. "No kidding! He used to work the line for you?"

"Oh, yeah. Most everyone ya see around here used to work the line for me, except the old farts and the women. You're the first girl I ever had working the line. That's how they all got their start." He liked to say that, as if it justified the minimum wage he paid.

Leo was a Boeing 727 flight engineer for Eastern Airlines. He showed up now and then in his crisp blue uniform to visit Rod. I could not imagine he'd gone the whole distance from driving the fuel truck and humping a fuel hose at Beverly to flying for Eastern. My hopes and plans for the airlines were reaffirmed.

"So you've been looking through seven years of cigar smoke. I probably could have backed the truck up a dozen times in front of these windows, and you'd never have known." He chewed on his cigar without acknowledging me, still staring out the windows. I went back to cleaning.

The next day, Steve and I arrived at the airport with a backpack full of clothes and supplies, some flight gear under my arm, and sunglasses. Steve had a tent and two sleeping bags. This weekend's guests would camp in tents or trucks while Rod's family stayed in the small cottage.

I went straight to Eighty-Delta, one of the Piper Warriors, with my stuff, and Steve went to Six-Mike-Mike. That was Rod's prized Cessna 172. They were tied down next to each other. I looked back through the clean glass and saw the office full of familiar faces getting ready to head to Vermont.

My fellow lineman Adam came out to meet me as I finished the pre-flight. He pushed his bag into the rear compartment with my things. It was heavy, and the clunk of a bottle as he set it down told me Adam was just going to be a passenger and not doing any of the flying today, even if he wanted to. It would just be the two of us in the plane.

Steve took off first, I followed, and Jerry Kennedy took off last in another of Rod's Warriors. The three planes congregated over Plum Island to the north at three thousand feet, and we continued north in loose formation. Steve's Cessna was ahead and to my left, while Jerry was ahead and to my right. Jerry's passengers were his girlfriend and his brother and his girlfriend.

The skies were clear, and the wind was light. I tuned the radio to 123.45 as we had agreed before takeoff and waited to hear Steve and Jerry's voices. It would be a two-hour flight to the Whitefield Airport in New Hampshire, and from there, Rod's camp was just over the Vermont line.

After establishing communication on the frequency, I fell silent while setting power and trim to maintain the formation. For days, I had been concerned about this flight. Of the three pilots, I was the least experienced and the least confident to take the airplane to its performance limits, which I knew Steve would not hesitate to do today. But I also saw this as an opportunity to show him I could fly as well as he did.

Steve's voice came over the frequency. Its sound was foreign even though it had been so close the night before. The voices went back and forth over the radio, talking and laughing with brief lulls as the other two airplanes mocked a dog fight with each other, peeling off left and right, down and under and from behind. Adam had already pulled the bottle from his backpack and started drinking as he watched the others.

"Eighty-Delta, you still with us? Haven't heard anything from you back there," Steve's voice resounded over the radio. "I think we'll take it up to sixty-five-hundred feet now. How 'bout it?"

"I'm with you," I answered. Until now, I had kept pace with them, though far enough behind to not require my participation. My flying confidence did not include interaction with other airplanes in the sky, so I was perfectly happy to fly behind the others.

"Move off to my left side, and we'll climb from there," he instructed.

Jerry entered the conversation. "I'm taking a more easterly route than you guys. I'll see you at Rod's." He turned to the right and went on his way.

I boosted the power as they eased back and positioned myself to the left of Six-Mike-Mike. We leveled at 6,500 feet.

"Hey, Beth, why don't you show Adam a roll. You have enough altitude," Steve suggested over the radio.

I hesitated for a moment and then asked Adam, "Have you ever done a roll?"

He put the bottle between his legs. "No, I can't say I have." His cheeks were already red from the booze. "Go for it!"

I took a deep breath, wondering how good a decision this was. But I was already committed when Steve suggested it. I needed to show him I was confident. "Okay, here goes," I announced over the radio. My intention had been tentative, but my voice was positive. The adrenaline began pumping through my body.

"Alright!" came Steve's response, and the voices of his passengers were yelling in the background. My determination escalated with Steve's enthusiasm. I had to do it.

"Ready?" I asked Adam, though the question was more for myself. He screwed the cap back onto his bottle. "You shouldn't need to do that if I pull this off okay," I told him, remembering Steve told me it was a one-G maneuver. Adam promptly removed the cap and lifted the bottle to his mouth.

Steve moved his Cessna ahead of me. Eighty-Delta was the slower of the two. With little in my mind except the maneuvers I remembered from that evening over the ocean, I began.

Power back, nose down, increasing speed, one hundred knots, one ten, one twenty, at the bottom of the yellow caution range now…my hand on the throttle, power back up to 2,400 RPM. My eyes were outside, sun glaring across the windows. I pulled back on the yoke and forced it to the right. Power, opposite rudder, full right aileron. We were over the top and in the middle of it, now inverted. But the aileron and rudder weren't taking me through the other half as they were supposed to. The airplane was falling out of the roll in the inverted position, violently losing altitude and winding up airspeed beyond red line as the nose pointed downward.

My hands and feet moved through all possible combinations. My mind was timelessly suspended in the inversion while my body worked furiously to right it.

And then the smell of whiskey reached my nose.

———

I almost didn't notice landing at Whitefield, still dazed by the unsuccessful roll. Adam and I climbed out of the airplane. Steve had already landed and walked over to meet us. He had a grim look on his face as he quietly inspected Eighty-Delta's wings. "Amazing," he said, shaking his head slowly. "You know, you shouldn't be here right now."

The fear was far from leaving my body, and with those words, it returned with double force. I said nothing.

"I looked down," he continued, "and saw you a couple thousand feet below us and falling fast. With the sun's glare, it looked like your wings had folded up and you were going in." He looked into my eyes. "Be careful."

His concern offered little comfort. We got in the waiting car for the ride to Rod's camp.

———

I saw the grave look on Rod's face.

"They crashed on I-95 in New Hampshire. Flyin' low and hit some power lines. Crashed and burned," Rod said tersely, hanging up the phone in the cabin. He was extremely disturbed. It was one of his people, one of his planes. "Two of 'em are dead." He chewed on his cigar for a moment, then took it between his fingers. "I hope to hell they weren't drinking."

"Jerry?" Steve's look showed true concern for the second time today.

Rod shook his head. "No, his brother and some girl they had with them. There were four of 'em."

Jerry and Steve were good friends. Jerry typically drank a lot and said little. I looked at Steve's face as he spoke, possibly detecting emotion.

"Then we almost lost two planes today," Steve said under his breath but loud enough to hear.

Rod looked over at him. "What are you talking about?"

"Nothing, Rod."

Steve looked at me briefly. I tried not to notice, just wanting to forget about it. Somehow, somewhere, in the inverted dive, I had found the right controls to force it out, but not before the airspeed had long since exceeded the never-exceed speed, the red line. We lost over two thousand feet, and Adam's shirt was soaked with whiskey, but he was too drunk to know that what might have ended disastrously had ended safely.

Not for Jerry, though. The National Transportation Safety Board (NTSB) reports would later tell us the aircraft was flying low at approximately one hundred feet above the ground when it collided with a high-tension cable, severing the left wing. Two of the passengers, Jerry's brother and his brother's girlfriend, were killed in the crash on Interstate 95. Jerry was found lying on the road when emergency crews arrived. The fourth passenger was still in the aircraft with the two dead bodies. His blood alcohol level was approximately 0.15 percent. Four months after they released him from the hospital, Jerry would be indicted for manslaughter. In April 1989, he was convicted on two counts of voluntary manslaughter and sentenced to two consecutive sentences, each from five to ten years.

I would never see Jerry again.

CHAPTER 7

Adam

It was still dark when the phone rang, and it woke me from a deep sleep. The red digits on my alarm clock glared 5:32. I reached from under the covers and reluctantly closed the distance between the warm bed and the cold phone.

"Hello?"

There was the sound of a clearing throat, and then, "Yeah, Beth, Rod here." He cleared his throat again. "I need ya to do something. You awake?"

"Uh huh."

"Adam Kraft did a number last night. Got himself drunk with some friends and took four of 'em flyin' in one of the Warriors. They went into the office and stole the keys to the new leaseback I've got and went for a joy ride." His voice was remarkably calm, like only a seasoned pilot could manage. "Ended up in Portland. Maine. Didn't know where the hell they were, and the tower up there had Adam arrested on the taxiway."

"Five grown men in a four-person plane?" Now I was fully awake.

"Yup. It's a damn shame is what it is. He'll lose all his licenses and ratings for this. What you need to do, hon, is get right over to the airport and take Five-Two-Five up to Portland and bail him out of jail. Adam's father's gonna meet ya at the airport with the money and the information y'll need to find him."

"Shouldn't someone go with me to fly the other Warrior home?" I wondered why he called me for this flight and not Steve.

"Not today. FAA and local police got the plane grounded until the owner decides if he's pressin' charges. He probably won't, but for now we gotta play by the rules. Besides, Steve's got students today. Alright, hon, get yourself over to the airport and call me when you get up to Portland."

"Alright. See ya later." I hung up the phone, shocked at what Adam had done. Rod's attention felt good. He had chosen me for the task. Meanwhile, I would be in Portland before Steve even found out the details of where I had gone and why. Rod was treating me as a legitimate, independent pilot, not just Steve's student or the lineperson.

———

I had never seen the inside of a prison before. My only images came from movies and television, and they were close to what I saw in Portland that morning. The taxi left me at a grouping of unmarked doors that was neither the front nor the rear of the large concrete building. I wove my way through a hallway to where a gray-haired woman sat behind bullet-proof glass with a large silver microphone in front of her face.

"I need to bail someone out." I hoped it was obvious I had never done this before.

"You want to see the prisoner first or pay the bail?" she asked.

"Uh, I guess I'll bail him out first."

"Okay," she said into the microphone and then swiveled her chair around. "Morty!" she yelled. A portly man in uniform appeared behind her. "Take her to the bail and bond room," she instructed him as she swiveled back around. "Morty'll escort you."

She buzzed Morty through the door, and he motioned for me to follow him. It was a long walk through bleak corridors to the bail and bond room. He did not speak, and the only sound was the echo of his shoes on the concrete floor. Morty waited by the door while I filled out paperwork and paid the bail at another desk shielded by glass.

"Someone here to see Prisoner Kraft," he said into the intercom.

The door buzzed, and Morty opened it for me. "You have fifteen minutes with him. I'll be waiting here for you."

"I just paid the bail," I said. "Can't he come out with me now?"

"No, they gotta do paperwork before they let him out through another door with his belongings," he explained impatiently. "He'll meet ya back down the hall where ya came in."

I walked through the door into a large open room with folding tables and chairs scattered around. Prisoners, mostly young and middle-aged men, sat with their Sunday morning visitors talking quietly while guards watched from the perimeter. I scanned the room and finally found Adam sitting at an empty table, leaning forward in his chair. He looked up as the door banged shut.

I walked over and put my hand on his shoulder. "How're you doing?" I sat in the chair next to him, hardly knowing what else to say.

Adam shook his head slowly. His dark, curly hair was uncombed, and his face showed a day's growth, making him look older than his twenty years. He looked at me pitifully with bloodshot eyes.

"I fucked up this time, Beth. I really fucked up." He shook his head again, close to tears, and leaned forward.

"You're still drunk, aren't you?"

"Yeah, a little."

"Do you remember what happened?"

"Sort of."

"Where are the others who were with you?"

"They jumped out of the plane on the taxiway and ran." His voice was plaintive, and it cracked as tears filled his eyes. "We landed without talking to anyone. I didn't have any idea where we were. Not even what state we were in." He dropped his head into his hands and began crying, knowing his dream of being an airline pilot had been dashed with one terrible decision.

There was nothing I could say. He was right. He fucked up. But then I thought of other times when I saw him drink to excess and wondered if something like this was bound to happen at some point.

I looked at my watch. There was no point prolonging this. "I've bailed you out," I said. "You'll be meeting me at the exit, and then we'll take a taxi back to the airport. I flew up in Five-Two-Five."

He nodded. I walked away, and the guard took Adam back through the opposite door. Morty was waiting for me at the entrance.

By the time we were airborne, clouds obscured the sky. Not low clouds, just enough to keep me on and off the instruments at cruising altitude. Since I had received my instrument rating, these were the first clouds I found myself in as pilot in command. I remained steady and calm, knowing from the weather briefer that it was a very mild case of instrument flight rules from Portland to Beverly.

Adam slept the entire way, still sobering up. The slight bump of our wheels touching the runway woke him, and he rubbed his head as we taxied to the ramp.

"Hey, Adam, your father will probably be here," I told him. He was looking out the window and did not answer.

As we opened the door to the office, Rod and Adam's father were waiting for us. His father's body language spoke to the disappointment he was feeling. Adam approached him. They said nothing and walked out together.

"Old man's kinda broken up. Wants to know where he went wrong," Rod said. "How'd the flight go? I see you got him bailed out alright."

"Yeah, everything was fine. A little IFR on the way home," I responded, still wondering where Steve was. He wasn't flying, and there were no other planes missing from the line.

"How 'bout a nip?" Rod offered. It was four o'clock, and he had already started.

"No, thanks." I leaned against the display case where Rod sold his aviation accessories. "So where is everyone?"

"Gone home, I imagine." He threw a small amount of V.O. down his throat. "Students got done early today 'cause we knew it was goin' IFR. Everyone else…well, it's just a quiet day."

"Mind if I use the phone?"

"Not if it's local."

Steve's number rang and rang. "Do you know where Steve is?" I asked as I hung up the phone.

"Like I said, I thought he went home. He was pretty tired when he left, said he was gonna get some sleep."

"Well, I guess I'll get going." I grabbed my flight bag. "See you tomorrow, Rod."

"Yup."

I went back the way Steve had shown me, through Beverly and over Kernwood Bridge into Salem. This time I did not ask myself if I should pass by his house to see if his car was in front. I would go there and ring the doorbell, probably waking him up. He wouldn't mind.

I turned down his street, passing the line of dreary homes. His was a green one with a chain-link fence around it, no garage, and a front porch enclosed with jalousie windows. It was no different from the other ones on the street, but Steve's green Pacer was not there.

It was not what I expected. I rolled to the end of the street and sat dumbly for a moment at the stop sign wondering what to do. An instant later, I turned left and sped to the main road. I would go to see if he was at Harriet's.

She lived in an apartment in a small town by the ocean. Steve and I had been there together for a summer party once. We didn't stay long, but its location was set in my mind. I knew the roads to get there, that it was on Magnolia Street, that it was apartment number one, that the house was yellow, the carpet was brown, the sofa was old, and the kitchen was dirty. I remembered too much about a place and a person who should not have mattered at all. But it did matter, too much, and I already hated myself for allowing this trip to Magnolia Street to happen.

The clouds thickened, and it began to rain. I thought about turning around and forgetting this nonsense but, with a singular fixation, I continued, leaving all self-respect somewhere back in Beverly. As the miles wound up—it was not a short drive—I tortured my mind. The bile rose in my throat. Turning off the main route onto Magnolia Street, I knew the answer was just a moment ahead of me. I swallowed hard, took a deep breath, and closed my eyes for an instant. Around one more curve, and there it was. The yellow house, and in the driveway only one car, Harriet's car.

I pulled to the side of the road in front of the house before Harriet's. The dividing row of shrubs concealed my car. I looked again and let out a deep sigh. There was no green Pacer in that driveway, nor in any driveway on the street. I did this to protect myself from future wounds that might be lurking. If Steve's car had been there, I would be obligated to break up with him to avoid being blind-sided by him breaking up with me. It was a defense mechanism I had been honing since Daddy died. If I was always on alert for disappointment or tragedy, then it would surely lessen the pain.

My breath quickened, and I threw open the car door and leaned out, vomiting into the gutter.

CHAPTER 8

On Skis

Snow blew across the ramp and into my face with irritating persistence. It was piled four feet high at the edges of the runways and taxiways from weeks of on-and-off storms. Between storms, Rod expected us to fly with our students, even if they didn't want to. The fact was that we needed to fly with our students in hopes that the weekly paycheck might top the previous weeks' checks of fifty or sixty dollars. Ten dollars an hour only while the prop was spinning made it difficult to earn a living in the winter.

I had passed my instructor rating flight test the day before Thanksgiving, just before the snow began to fall. Steve and Tim were the senior instructors on Rod's line and had the most students, but even they were struggling to make a living during the winter months. As the newest flight instructor at New England Flyers, with a total of only 370 hours, I continued working the line for the steady paycheck as I waited to get some students. Rod took care of me as much as he could, but it was not much while the snow kept piling up.

The preheater provided the only chance for flying on days like this. With a temperature of five degrees and no hope for

much over fifteen or twenty as the day progressed, Cherokees and Warriors could hardly turn their props without help. The ancient little machine known as the preheater was Rod's lifeline in the winter. And the instructors'. And the airplanes'.

I put the heat nozzle into the left engine intake of Five-Two-Five and grappled with the rest of the contraption to keep it from falling apart. What we had was a propane tank mounted on wheels, fueled by a flame lit by an igniter. Somewhere involved in all of this was a blower at the base of a piece of dryer hose that I stuffed into the engine intake, one side at a time, twenty minutes per side, always attended. From the way the preheater was held together with a couple of coat hangers and electrical tape, I imagined Rod had given a previous lineman a picture of a real preheater and told him to devise one as a solution to Rod's wintertime blues.

Once the engine was preheated, a few pulls through of the propeller, and it was ready to start. But it didn't always happen that way, and Steve would have to hand prop it. It was a risky task when the ramp was icy—the force needed to throw the prop of a 160-horsepower was significant. I tried it only once and learned the Cub's hundred-horse engine was about all I could handle.

I looked over at the Cub in her tie-down spot on the grass, bright yellow against the white snow, and thought about the day ahead. Rod had selected me for the important mission of taking the Cub to New Hampshire to fit it with skis, getting checked out to fly with skis, and then returning with her to Beverly. For the Cub Club members, getting outfitted with skis was the most exciting event since her arrival in the summer. All this was to happen while Steve flew with his students. It was my job alone, and I asked Melanie Sullivan, one of the newest members of the Cub Club and my first private pilot student, to join me on the mission.

By the time I had completed all the needed preheats, Melanie arrived at the airport. Together, we loaded the skis into the Cub's tail compartment and took off for Hampton Airfield, a small grass strip by the coast.

In her late thirties and divorced with no children, Melanie was an attractive blonde who allowed no limits on her life. Which was why she divorced her attorney-husband. He would not go skydiving with her, and that was where the end of the marriage began. She had been doing all she wanted with no regrets ever since, and the latest was learning to fly.

One day in the late fall, before we met, Melanie had watched from the side of the road as I practiced landings in the Cub on the grass strip at Plum Island Airport. She decided immediately the Cub was for her. Melanie bought the tenth share and became my first student.

The Cub touched down softly on the packed snow that was Hampton Airfield's runway. Snow almost guaranteed soft landings, and it was gratifying. I did a one-eighty on the runway and taxied to the little cluster of World War II–era buildings. Hampton was a grass strip that opened in 1945, offering flight training and sales of Piper aircraft, Piper Cubs in particular. The field probably didn't look much different in 1945 than it did now. There were period aircraft lined up in front. The flight school building hadn't seen new paint in years, nor had the maintenance hangar, a Quonset-style hut. Here, the Cub was one of many. Hampton's flight school used at least half a dozen of them as trainers, and in the winter, they were all on skis, as ours would soon be.

The mechanic met us as the propeller came to a halt. "You here from Rod's?" he asked.

"That's us. We've got the skis in the back." I climbed out from the back seat and pulled skis and hardware from the rear compartment.

"Roger." He was flustered. I assumed that response meant that his name was Roger and not the radio response *Roger*. "This shouldn't take more than an hour or two. You can wait in the office." He wanted us to leave him alone to do the job.

Instead, we borrowed the airport car, a big, old car, not unlike Rod's shitbox, and drove up US Route One to a diner in town for breakfast.

"What's this I hear about you seeing a guy named Steve? Is it the Steve I've seen around the airport? An instructor, also flies the Cub?"

I nodded.

"Really? You're not serious?" she asked, making me squirm.

"What do you mean?" I asked defensively.

"You know what I mean. Come on, Beth, he's nothing special." Her eyes showed an obvious enjoyment with this. Our brief friendship so far comprised flying lessons and occasionally getting together for coffee. "From what I've seen, he has no personality, no money, and he's not even that good to look at."

I concentrated on my tea.

"What is it? Because he's your instructor?" Melanie got right to the point and hit all the nails on the head. "How cliché! There're better things for you." My continued lack of reaction would not deter her. "I'll think of some way to get you to move on. In fact, I already have some ideas."

I raised my eyebrows. "Oh? Like what?" I asked skeptically.

"I have to give it more thought. Don't worry, though," she smiled. "I'll let you know when the time is right."

Melanie wouldn't go any further for now, which was fine with me. I stood slowly, muscles sore from the night before, and headed toward the bathroom.

"Why are you walking funny?" she asked when I came back.

"I went running last night."

"In the snow?"

"Yeah," I admitted. "Steve read an article about the importance of aerobic exercise, so he wants to start running every day."

She laughed, perhaps at me. "Why does that mean you have to go with him?"

"We had dinner together at my place last night, so what was I supposed to do when he decided to go? I had no choice."

"Of course you had a choice."

I suddenly realized how stupid it was not to just stay back and do something else the night before.

"Well, I thought I could use the exercise," I said. "He decided he wanted to follow the old train tracks that run down the street. Those tracks go on for a long way, all the way into Swampscott." I paused for a moment. "After about twenty minutes, I couldn't keep up with him, but he wouldn't slow down or even stop." I sipped my tea. "So he kept going. We were out for a couple of hours, and I spent the whole miserable time just trying to keep up with him."

She shook her head. "He's a jerk, and you're stupid."

"Thanks, Melanie. That makes me feel good. Don't forget I'm your flight instructor. Have a little respect," I said only half joking.

"You know exactly what I mean."

I looked away. It was as much acknowledgement as I could give. What she said was harsh but true, and it embarrassed me. How had I gotten to this point? Had I lost all self-respect?

The waitress interrupted my thoughts when she brought out over-easy eggs, toast, and bacon for both of us. I poured more tea into my mug and changed the subject. "I've been thinking of some places to take the Cub once spring comes. The skis are going on it now, but that'll only last as long as the snow, two or three months at the most. How about we go on a trip overnight somewhere?"

"Atlantic City," she replied, not looking up from her food.

"Atlantic City? Have you been thinking about this?"

"No, but I know it would be fun."

I laughed at her never-ending confidence. I also admired it. Something to learn from.

"What's the matter? Don't you think it would be a good place to go with the Cub?"

I nodded my head. "Yeah, I think it would be great." I thought for a minute and added, "Here's what we'll do—we'll fly down the Hudson River through the VFR corridor. Then we can circle the Statue of Liberty." Now I was getting excited.

"What's the VFR corridor?"

"It's a strip of uncontrolled airspace over the Hudson River alongside New York City—you can fly through it under visual flight rules, you know, when the weather is clear, without dealing with air traffic controllers. Helicopters use it most, but small planes can use it, too. You just have to stay low."

She put down her fork. "Alright, then it's a plan. As soon as the Cub is back on her wheels."

My checkout ride on skis was the last step before we could return to Beverly. The only instructor at Hampton that morning sat behind the desk reading a book on how to become an airline pilot. Flying with me meant more money in his paycheck and another hour in his logbook, so he quickly closed the book and followed me out to the Cub.

After thirty minutes, I could successfully handle her on skis for taxi, takeoff, and landing, and it satisfied the instructor. It had been easy. Melanie and I took off for the flight home.

"Beverly Tower, Cub Four-Four-Three-Four-Tango seven miles northeast, with Sierra," I called in when we were in range. "Requesting a low pass over the east side of Runway 16 followed by a left pattern to landing."

"Roger, Three-Four-Tango, report left base for the low pass," came the reply.

Rod had asked me to do a low pass over New England Flyers to let him know we had returned and give him time to come out and watch. Some Cub Club members were there waiting, and Steve would be there watching me fly the airplane, hopefully this time not critically as an instructor, but with excitement.

"Three-Four-Tango, cleared for the low pass."

I descended to two hundred feet on final and then a little more for the pass. Low passes were always a thrill, and this one especially so. At full Cub speed, which was not quick, I overflew the area where we would land next time around. We buzzed by the control tower at their window height and then turned sharply over the flight school building. Six or seven people stood outside the office with their heads turned up to see. I pushed the throttle forward for the climb to the pattern altitude of one thousand feet and called in the downwind leg to the tower. They cleared me to land. Rod had already made arrangements with the control tower for us to land the Cub to the left of that runway. It was a snow-covered area about two thousand feet long.

I touched down softly and taxied the remaining distance to the end. This was where the Cub would reside for the next few months.

I saw Steve through the windshield holding a camera in his hands. He stood next to an older man, his father. Rod stood by, his hands in his pockets and an afternoon smile on his face. They shot a few pictures before moving aside for me to taxi up. I shut down the engine, and we climbed out.

"It's a lot of fun, isn't it?" Steve asked as I emerged. His excitement was obvious as his eyes still focused on the airplane.

"It's great. Best flying I've done so far."

"How is the fuel?" He checked the floater gauge behind the engine. "Good enough. I'm going up."

"Alone?" I asked.

"Yeah," he answered and climbed in. Rod propped him on the first try.

I walked over to where Melanie was standing on the snow and watched Steve maneuver the Cub as effortlessly as he did a Cherokee, no coaching requested or required. Melanie grabbed my arm and dragged me away toward the parking lot. I stopped to look back at the sun fading behind the trees on the other side of the airport. Steve had taken off and was coming around for his own first landing on skis.

CHAPTER 9

Atlantic City

We got a late start to Atlantic City on that sunny day in mid-April. By the time Melanie and I went out to pre-flight the Cub, it was already after two o'clock. The main tank, the only usable tank on the Cub, was full. She also had wing tanks that fed into the main tank behind the engine firewall, but Rod suspected they were contaminated, so we never used them. Because the airplane had no electrical system, the fuel gauge was a simple floater gauge—a wire attached to a cork in the tank threaded through the gas cap. The less wire you saw, the less fuel you had.

"Everything looks good. You ready to go?" I asked Melanie, my back to her. There was no answer. I turned to see she was back on the other side of the ramp talking and laughing with Tim, her arms moving along with her mouth.

"Melanie!" I yelled. "Let's go!"

She threw up her arms and ran back to the airplane. "Okay, okay! Are we ready?"

"Get in and I'll prop it," I said.

By two thirty, we were finally in the air. With our overnight bags and gear stashed in the rear, I flew backseat, and Melanie flew front seat. When we reached our altitude of three thousand feet and heading of two hundred degrees, I leaned forward.

"You fly and I'll navigate," I said. "This heading is good for now."

She nodded. I unfolded my chart and inspected the pencil line I had drawn for the course to the Hudson River.

"We'll have to stop for fuel and overnight long before Atlantic City," I said over her shoulder. "But I'd like to get through New York and the corridor before we do, then stop for the night in New Jersey." Melanie nodded again.

I looked at the wet compass mounted above the instrument panel, then at my chart, and then at the ground. "Turn a little further right."

The Cub was always a seat-of-your-pants flying experience. Our only guides were the terrain, the charts, and a wet compass riddled with error. Even a Cherokee was a high-tech affair next to the Cub.

The sky was clear, and the horizon as unobscured as could be. The visibility went on for miles; the navigation required little effort. To conserve the handheld radio's inadequate battery power, I steered our course above and around the controlled fields in our path. Progress was slow with opposing winds, and I spent my time fine-tuning our heading for wind correction.

By four thirty, we approached the Hartford area, almost halfway to the Tappan Zee Bridge, which spanned the Hudson River. I still didn't want to have to use the radio, but it would be inevitable unless we dipped southward off the course I was trying to follow. I glanced out the windshield for a fuel check. The wire had sunk about four inches as nearly as I could estimate, with five or so to go.

After Hartford, the towns passed quickly. Meriden, Ansonia, the northern part of Bridgeport. By Wilton, the sun had disappeared, and a chill penetrated the fabric walls of the Cub's fuselage. I checked the fuel for the first time since Hartford and saw that the wire had gone down another couple of inches in that time. I weighed the distance we still planned to fly, the amount of fuel we may or may not have had, and the dwindling daylight hours, and knew I had to come up with an alternate plan. Without an electrical system, we had no lights—no instrument panel lights, no landing lights, and, most significantly, no aircraft position lights. Without those, we could not legally or easily fly or land after sunset.

The sinking sun ahead on the horizon was reminding me that our time would be up soon. I decided we would cross the Hudson north of the Tappan Zee and land there. To avoid being written up by a tower controller for a possible violation, the only option was to land at an uncontrolled airport. I studied the chart already memorized in my head and crossed off the airfields on the east side of the river. White Plains ahead, Danbury to the north. I then crossed off the controlled fields on the west side. I didn't want to consider turning back to Waterbury and losing ground.

Along the west side of the river and almost straight ahead, I identified Ramapo Valley Airport on the map in the Spring Valley area of New York. Twenty-five-hundred feet of paved runway and fuel available.

I tapped Melanie on the shoulder. "I've got the airplane now," I told her and took control of the stick. "We need to land soon. You see the fuel gauge?"

Melanie nodded.

"It's going down faster every time I look at it. Not only that, the sun's on its way down, and it's going to get dark fast. We can't land at a controlled field," I continued.

She nodded again.

My voice was getting tired. "Take out your copy of the New York chart."

I sat back and flew while she opened her map. The sky was dusky, but not dark yet. We would definitely land with plenty of light by taking a direct course to Ramapo Valley. To do that, I needed to turn the radio on to get clearance through the White Plains traffic area.

"I have to turn the radio on," I told Melanie, "but I'm planning on landing at this airport right here." I pointed to it on her map. "Ramapo Valley. They have fuel there."

I tuned the radio to the tower frequency. "Westchester Tower, Cub Four-Four-Three-Four-Tango, seven miles east at two thousand feet, requesting transition east to west."

"Roger, Three-Four-Tango, report clear." His transmission was short, and I caught it all despite the static.

The ten-mile transition was slow, made slower in my mind as I watched the daylight fade. I reported clear of the area and turned the radio off. The Hudson River lay ahead, and the Tappan Zee Bridge crossed it. My confidence was restored. Slow going as it was, we would soon be on the ground.

On the west side of the bridge, the New York State Thruway continued ahead. I flew a course parallel to the thruway at 1,500 feet, knowing Ramapo Valley would not be far from it. Just another seven or eight miles. Because the aeronautical charts eliminated most major road details in urban areas, the thruway was visible only in brief segments on the chart, and I could not pinpoint the airport's precise location in relation to it.

Both of us had our charts open on our laps, and both of us looked from one side of the airplane to the other waiting for Ramapo Valley or its beacon to appear. Where the thruway came back into view on the chart, it showed a ninety-degree turn to the north just beyond Spring Valley. When we reached that turn in the road with no sign of the airport yet, I turned around.

"We must have passed it," I yelled to Melanie. "It's just off the thruway."

She looked at her chart. "Maybe try a little further that way," she suggested, pointing south.

I veered a little to the south and flew a zig-zag course, scrutinizing every possibility for a runway. The visibility was poor with dusk fully upon us. When we reached the bridge again, I was getting nervous. Within a short time, we would be in the darkness of night, aided only by city lights. And those would not help us find a landing site.

"How about just going to this airport?" Melanie showed me another uncontrolled field about fifteen miles away.

"No fuel there," I said. "We've got to find this one, we're here now."

She threw her attention outside to resume the search as I covered a line slightly more southerly than the first two. As the daylight continued to diminish, my course was becoming irregular, circling the area where I was sure the airport should be.

Finally, I turned west again, sure I was missing something obvious. When the hills rose ahead of us and the city lights became sparse, I reversed direction once more and considered an emergency landing on a field or a road. At least now we had the luxury of choosing a location rather than being forced to take what was below us when the engine sputtered from fuel starvation. I circled the same area, refusing to accept that we couldn't find Ramapo Valley.

Melanie turned back and yelled, "Maybe we'd better just land on a field or something. This airport doesn't exist. Let's do it while—"

"There it is," I yelled. Dark as it was, the small airport with one runway and two taxiways popped into view. I immediately clicked the microphone seven times to activate the runway lights, but nothing happened. It remained dark.

I descended to approach the runway from the south. There would be no pattern here, just an expedited landing. As I turned final and lined up with the runway a half mile out, it became clear there was a reason the runway lights had not come on. Something was wrong, very, very wrong.

"Beth!" Melanie was pointing to the runway ahead.

I could see it now. The runway appeared broken up. I aborted the landing and went in for a low pass to take a closer look. It was difficult to make out, but as we approached, it became clear. The runway was torn apart. Bulldozed into hundreds of slabs of asphalt.

"What the fuck?!" Melanie shrieked.

I threw in full power and brought the Cub around to resume a final approach. There was no choice but to land. My adrenaline flowed as I lined up with the area to the right of the runway. Dirt, I thought. But no, not in the wet weather we'd been having. Mud. But that was still better than bulldozed asphalt.

This required a slow, three-point landing to keep the tail planted in the mud. Otherwise, we'd bog down and bury the nose. Because of the darkness, there was no way to judge when the plane would touch down. I should have maintained power all the way down, but I gambled that it was mud and forfeited the extra bit of power. In any case, a mud landing would be soft.

We came down to the threshold, and I gradually eased the stick back. The Cub set her wheels into the ground with a wet sound, coming to a quick halt. Yes, it was mud, and we were at least a few inches deep in it. I cut the engine and let out my breath. Finally, there was silence. My thoughts spiraled into panic as I considered the consequences, my mind racing with thoughts of violations, a wrecked airplane, and if or how we could get out of this mess. Any of these could mean a violation and a quick end to my dreams of the airlines.

"What the hell happened to the runway?" Melanie asked, emphasizing each word.

I shook my head. "I don't know what's going on," I replied, "but we're sitting here knee deep in mud."

"With no fuel and no way to fly out," Melanie added.

"No," I corrected her, "there's a way, just not an easy way. And we're going to have to try it."

"What's that?"

"The taxiway looked intact from the air."

"You're crazy."

"No, just desperate." I unlatched the door, and we climbed out. Sure enough, the mud was deep, about four or five inches. I walked about thirty feet to find the edge of the taxiway. "The taxiway is still intact," I called over to her. "And I can see a hangar behind those trees. With lights on."

I walked back to the airplane, sinking into the mud with each step. "We have to drag this thing out of the mud and onto the taxiway. Are you up for it?"

"Don't think we have a choice."

Melanie positioned herself behind the left wing strut while I lifted the tail out of the mud. We both pushed as hard as we could. After five feet, we stopped for a rest.

"Hey!" a voice called. "What's going on?"

"Oh, shit!" I swore. "If this is the police or the FAA, we're screwed. Let me do the talking."

I dropped the tail back down in the mud. It sank down with a wet, sucking sound. We walked to the narrow taxiway where two men in suits and trench coats were standing.

"What happened to the runway?" was all I could say.

"Bulldozed," one of the men said. "Just this afternoon, in fact, and the taxiways are scheduled for demolition tomorrow." He had a southern twang. "We saw you flying over and then a low pass with no lights. We weren't sure if you were having a problem or something, but then you landed. I thought for sure you'd busted up the airplane." He looked over at the Cub. "Would have been a shame. But you did a damn nice job putting it down with all these obstacles."

I relaxed a little, realizing these men were not FAA or cops.

The second man stepped forward. "You'll need help dragging it out of the mud." His accent was pure New Jersey.

"We sure do." Melanie did not hesitate to accept the help.

"I don't understand," I said, still in disbelief. "You said the runway was just bulldozed this afternoon. What's going on?"

"Well," the one from New Jersey said, "the airport is officially closed."

"I can see that."

"As of today," he continued, "it's just a heliport now. That's what the hangars are for, where we watched you from. We fly for a corporate helicopter fleet based here. The rest of this place is going to be condos. It's listed in the NOTAMs.[6]"

---

6   A NOTAM is a notice containing information essential to flight operations but not known far enough in advance to be publicized on the regular flight charts.

"Didn't you call Flight Service before we left?" Melanie asked me.

"Of course I did, but Ramapo Valley wasn't exactly on our itinerary today. It wouldn't even have been an alternate." Poor planning could end up shutting down my career goals. I had never considered alternate airports, fuel range and daylight, instead just winging the flight with little forethought for contingency plans. I wanted to blame Steve for being the one who taught me to cut corners, just as I was now showing to my student Melanie, but the sobering reality was I was the pilot in command here, not Steve.

"Let's get you pulled out of the mud and up onto the taxiway here. We'll push it down to the hangars and keep it there overnight. Don't want anyone to see a fixed wing sitting here. Might make the FAA curious enough to come and investigate."

I hesitated. "The big question is whether you have hundred low-lead fuel here. I imagine all the helicopters are turbine."

"Yeah, they are. But we can still fix you up with some good old low lead. No problem there."

We walked through the mud to where the Cub sat, looking rather pitiful. I glanced at the men's feet. Their shoes and pants were ruined, and it filled me with a combination of guilt and gratitude at the same time.

In a short time, we had the Cub on the narrow taxiway. From there, it sloped down to the hangar.

"We need to take off very early tomorrow," I said. "Right at sunrise. I don't want any airport neighbors calling the police or the FAA."

Our new southerner friend laughed. "Oh, I wouldn't worry too much about that, honey. You've got little tiny numbers on this here Cub. No one likely to pick those off it from the ground when you fly over."

"That's true," I answered. "But suppose the Feds show up here to ask the two of you about a little yellow airplane that flew in and took off? You couldn't deny it."

"Well, you haven't told us your names. And it's too dark to see those tiny, mud-covered numbers anyway. I guess we just wouldn't be much help." He winked and smiled. He and his friend were colluding with us as fellow pilots in this crazy world of civil aviation, just as we would do for them if the situation were reversed. We all had to look out for each other.

"Will you be here early in the morning? As early as we're talking about?" Melanie asked them.

"Sure will," came the answer.

"Okay," I said, "but how long is the taxiway? This whole conversation is pointless if we can't get off the ground."

"There's one taxiway worth using, and you were just on it. Runs parallel to the runway, but you only have maybe, well, three hundred feet," he estimated with a twang, "at the most."

Three hundred feet...at the most. Our adventures at Ramapo Valley were only half over. The flight out would be equally precarious, except that this time I had the whole night to think about it.

CHAPTER 10

Ramapo Valley

The hotel lounge in Spring Valley was like any other. We had our dinner in the restaurant—pretzels, free hors d'oeuvres, and Scotch. I wished the lights were dimmer and the music softer. My nerves needed a break. For Melanie, it was not as tense, and I understood why when I recalled some of the risky flights with Steve. He was pilot in command and held the real responsibility. And so it was this time with me, for the first time.

"Do you want to keep on going to Atlantic City?" Melanie asked.

"I say we head down the corridor. That was supposed to be the highlight of this trip," I reminded her. "Then we'll stop for breakfast and see where to go from there. Depends on the weather, too."

"That's true. If the weather goes bad on us, we may not even get out of here."

"That's not the only reason we may not get out of here."

The bartender refilled the pretzels. For a long while, we were silent.

"You know what words keep going through my head, over and over?" I shook my head as I relived seeing the destroyed runway. "They bulldozed the runway today!'"

"Stop talking about it," Melanie scolded me. "Forget it for now. There's another thing I want to talk to you about." She took a large swallow from her glass. "I've been thinking about your job. Flight instructing, I mean. I think it's time for you to do some other kind of flying. I have an idea. There's a banner-towing company at Lawrence Airport. You should get a job there."

"Melanie," I said, "you don't understand—this fuckup here at Ramapo Valley isn't over yet. If we don't get off the ground tomorrow, or if someone shows up and reports the plane between now and then, I'm screwed. It will go on my record as an incident or a violation."

"You'll be fine. Don't worry about it," she said lightly. "You need to advance your career."

"Every flight instructor in America wants to move on from flight instruction to get closer to the airlines. What makes you think I could get a job banner-towing with as little time as I have? I've only been an instructor for four months. Besides, I haven't taken you through to your private license yet."

She shook her head slowly, looking at me. "Forget that. You have plenty of taildragger time in the Cub. And that's all they fly for banner-towing—Cubs and Stearmans. Taildraggers. You're perfect for it."

"So what? Steve has a ton more time than I do."

"You're forgetting a few things here," she explained. "First, he hasn't done any looking, and second, you're a woman!" She smiled triumphantly as if telling me a secret.

I raised my eyebrows. "You're joking, right?"

"Of course not. This is aviation. There aren't many female pilots out there in your position. Take advantage of it. You're just as good as Steve, but because you're a woman, you have the edge. You know, that thing called equal opportunity."

She was way off base. This industry was run by men for men, and they didn't want to consider equal opportunity and quotas. Still, though, she had a good idea with the banner-towing. It would be a new challenge, a different kind of flying.

"Summer is coming. They're hiring. When do you think they fly most of their banners? But if you're not interested in that angle, then how about a job with an air charter company? You have your multi-engine rating."

"Yeah, I have the rating, but not enough hours for anyone to even look at me. Let's go back to the banner-towing. I'll send a resume."

"Oh, for God's sake, Beth, forget your college habits. This is aviation, and we're talking about a ma-and-pa business. Take your log book and walk into the office and say, 'My name is Beth Ruggiero, and I want to work for you'—just like that."

"They'll laugh me right off the airport."

She didn't answer, and I said nothing more. But I decided I would take her advice on this one.

———

I woke up early and went to the window to check the weather. The sun was a long way from rising, but I didn't see stars. At the horizon, though, the conditions looked possibly forgiving enough for us to take off. I woke Melanie, and we got ready to leave the hotel.

It was still dark when the taxi left us at the Ramapo Valley. We were quiet in anticipation of the flight out. The distant sound of the thruway was all I could hear as we approached the hangar. Our new friends had already pulled the Cub out of the hangar, and it was waiting for us on the small ramp. Inside the hangar, the lights were on, and one of the men was standing in the doorway drinking coffee.

"Howdy," he greeted us. "Y'all ready to try your luck?"

"I think so," I responded. "How can we get some of that fuel you were talking about?"

"It's all taken care of and ready to go. You've got five gallons besides what you had before."

I didn't mention that what we had before was not enough to make a difference, but he probably had already figured that out.

"I had the line guy spray it off real quick with the hose, got some of that mud cleaned off," he continued. "You should be all set to go. By the time you preflight and get it propped, there'll be enough daylight to get out of here."

I smiled at him with deep gratitude. If we were successful, we could never have pulled it off without their help.

"What I'd suggest you do is taxi up the hill there and then down to the end of the taxiway. Turn around at the end and take off in that direction." He pointed away from the city.

We would do as he suggested, but I knew keeping the plane on the narrow slice of pavement in the takeoff run would be tricky. I was concerned it would affect our ability to develop enough speed to get off the ground in the short distance.

We taxied to the end of the taxiway, and I pulled the throttle to idle.

"I'm getting out to lift the tail and swing it around," I told Melanie. "I want to make sure we're getting every possible inch."

"Okay," she said, "I'll hold the brakes."

I climbed from the back seat out the door.

"Hey," she yelled. I looked back over my shoulder. "Is this going to work?"

"Say some prayers. It might help."

It took all my strength to lift the tail, but a dose of adrenaline this morning made the task easier. I swung it around and pulled back as far as the pavement would allow. I surveyed the taxiway ahead and thought it over. We were light, with minimal fuel and baggage. Melanie and I combined were the weight of one slightly overweight man. It looked about 250 or 300 feet to the end, just as our friend had estimated, but there was no forgiveness at the end of the runway where it fell off abruptly. There was a five-story building about a quarter of a mile beyond that we would have to clear. If it wasn't for that building, I wouldn't have been too concerned. The problem was that the takeoff required standard short field procedure—hold the brakes until the throttle was all the way open, fifteen or twenty degrees of flaps for extra lift to get off the ground sooner, then keep it low and level in ground effect to build more speed for the climb. But the J-3 was not equipped with flaps, and these brakes were not likely to hold all the way to full power. If I didn't have enough speed to take off by the end, I may have to follow the downward slope of the ground to pick up more speed.

I climbed back in and took the controls. "You ready?" I asked. "As ever."

I held the brakes as firmly as possible and prayed they might be more reliable today than usual. With my left hand, I gradually slid the throttle forward. Too fast, and the brakes would never hold. At full throttle, I let her go, my feet active on the rudder pedals trying to keep our wheels on the pavement. We lumbered forward, gathering speed, and I pushed the stick forward to pull the tail off the ground. Speed came a little faster now, but it felt like a takeoff in slow motion.

"Shit!" I yelled when the left wheel veered off the side of the taxiway. I quickly corrected to the right. It happened again about two-thirds of the way, and I swore even louder as I jerked the airplane back on course. The end was coming up, and we were not ready to fly. *You've got to do it anyway*, I told myself and forced her off the ground. She stayed airborne, only dipping down a couple of feet as the ground dropped off below us. There still wasn't enough speed to climb or turn, and definitely not enough altitude to make it over the building ahead. In that fraction of a second, I looked at the downward slope below us knowing it was our only hope. I pushed the stick forward, and we followed the terrain down to where it leveled, gaining speed. It wasn't a long slope, but just enough that by the time we got to the bottom, I'd have enough speed to do a climbing turn. We resurfaced at the top of the opposite side of the incline, once again in view of the hangar and the bulldozed runway, and were able to climb to a safe altitude to clear the building ahead. I wiped the sweat from my forehead.

CHAPTER 11

Banners

"I won't be teaching for you anymore, Rod."

The office was empty and quiet. Rod sat on his stool behind the counter, the afternoon sun shining on his face as he watched the ramp outside. Whiskey time had begun two hours earlier. He shifted an expressionless gaze from the ramp to where I was standing by the counter.

"I got a job towing banners over at Lawrence Airport," I announced.

"Yeah? For Brian Patterson?" he asked.

I nodded.

"You given it much thought?" he asked.

"Enough to know I want to give it a try."

He turned his attention back to the ramp outside. There still was no expression on his face, but I knew he had more to say.

"Banner-towin' is a hell of a dangerous thing, ya know," he said slowly. "Aside from crop dustin', it's some of the most dangerous flyin' there is."

I remained quiet, listening to his words and knowing Rod well enough to know his concerns were real. Others may have told me he just didn't want to lose a flight instructor just before the busy summer season. That was partially true, but not entirely, and I listened.

"Have ya had any trainin' yet?" he asked.

"Just one time up in one of the Super Cubs[7] with Brian."

"You seen actual pickups?" He was referring to the heart of the maneuver—picking up the banner from the ground.

I nodded.

"And you know about Brian's track record?"

"No. What do you mean?"

Rod relit yesterday's cigar and shook his head. "Well, it ain't too good. You oughta know that. He loses a pilot at the rate of almost one a year. And I don't mean because they quit. You don't see that happenin' in no flight school. Hell, it was just last year he had an accident himself." His blue eyes were serious as he looked at me. "He came out of it okay, but that girl who was in the same accident, now she's got problems for life."

I recalled the girl in the wheelchair in Brian's office when I applied for the job. She was attached to an intravenous drip. Rod must have meant her. "I saw her. What happened?"

"Oh, Jesus, I don't know for sure," he said. "What I heard was that they were flyin' the Stearmans side by side for a parallel banner pickup. Her banner got tangled up in Brian's banner, and they both crashed. But that wasn't the first accident, and it sure as hell ain't gonna be the last. When you come down to forty or fifty feet to hook a sign layin' on the ground and then gotta gain a few hundred feet of altitude in ten or fifteen seconds with all that drag on the tail, you're just lookin' for trouble. If your engine dies with that sign danglin' off your tail, then you're goin' down fast and hard."

---

7   The Super Cub and J-5 Cub were later variants of the J-3 Cub. They had flaps, electrical system, and wider fuselage, and the pilot sat in the front seat rather than the back. The Stearman is a biplane that was introduced in 1934 as a military training aircraft and more powerful than the Cubs.

He had my attention, and I was listening closely.

"Every now and then," he continued, "I get someone calling to ask for a banner tow. Birthday, marriage proposal, whatever. I'll take the job, do it in my Cessna, but I never have one of my instructors do the job. Too damn risky." He went into the back room where the bottle was and refilled his paper cup. "You think real hard about it, honey. It's some risky flyin'."

He had said all he had to say and, except for the occasional sound of an airplane taking off or landing, the office was once again silent.

———

"How'd you manage that?" Steve asked when I told him the news.

"I walked in, told him my name and that I wanted to work for him." I was proud of my answer and inwardly thanked Melanie for the inspiration.

"That's it?" he said flatly.

"Well, no. The owner sent me up for a test flight in the Super Cub with one of the pilots. I did fine, and he gave me a job. *That's* it."

"Why didn't you tell me you before you went? I would've gone, too."

I shrugged without looking at him. "I don't know, didn't think you'd be interested," I lied.

We sat on the couch in the family room at his father's house. The television was on, the evening news. The room was dark and gloomy as always, even with the lights on. Steve's father spent most of his time in this room, drinking coffee and watching television, and only shifted from the couch to the kitchen and back again. This evening, though, we were alone in the house, and it was the first chance to tell him I wouldn't be teaching for Rod anymore. I had kept it a secret until now in what was likely a futile effort to eliminate any competition from him.

Steve's attention moved back to the television. A multi-car accident on Route 128 north of Boston was causing rush-hour headaches. I pretended to be interested in what the anchorman was reporting. When the news ended, Steve asked, "Have you had any training yet?"

I glanced from the television to see his expression before answering. "Uh huh. Been up twice, about an hour each time. We've been simulating the pickup. Next time or two, we'll do actual pickups, and then I'll be on my own with it." I paused to see his reaction. There was none. "I'll be flying over Fenway when the Red Sox are playing. And up and down Revere Beach." I wished I could conceal my excitement at the prospect of this new job, but it was useless to try. "He starts everyone out in the Cubs—Super Cubs and J-5s, a hundred and eighty horsepower. If you stay with him long enough, and you're good enough, you get to fly one of the Stearmans.

Those are the biplanes with the huge rotary engines."

"He's still hiring, huh?"

"I guess so," I responded reluctantly.

"You want something to eat? I'm ordering a pizza."

"Sure."

He went to use the phone in the kitchen, closing the discussion on banner-towing. I heard him order a large with peppers and onions, the two things I disliked most on a pizza, which he knew but chose to either forget or ignore.

I was proud to have made this step to a new job at a different airport on my own and somehow hoped Steve would recognize and praise my accomplishment. My deep need for male approval, or in this case, Steve's approval, had consumed me since losing my father. Still, how foolish to think it would happen here. Steve and I were both pilots seeking the same ultimate airline goal, and for Steve, his sole instinct was to advance toward that goal by whatever means possible. Not only were we in a relationship, but now we were also in competition, so I hated divulging everything about my new job. He would probably pursue the same job with the same company the next day.

I nestled into the deep couch cushions seeking comfort, for the first time appreciating the darkness of the room.

———

Melanie and I sat on the grass next to the taxiway. From there, we could watch Brian's planes taxi out, pick up their banners, drop them, and land. We drove to Lawrence Airport this sunny day in her MG Midget. It was the car's first day out for the season, with the top down, and as soon as I told her the news of my job, she headed to Lawrence to see what I'd be flying.

"It went just as you said," I said. "Thanks for the push."

She laughed. "I just told you to try. But what's this about Steve. Or do I not want to know?"

"You don't want to know," I confirmed.

"Tell me anyway."

"What's there to tell? I told him I got a job here. How could I not have told him?" I said defensively. "He asked a bunch of questions, the last of which was, 'Is Brian still hiring?' Next thing I know, he's gotten a job here, too. I couldn't stop him from doing what he wanted, and even if I could, I don't know if I would. He's part of my life."

"Yeah, I know. A bad part." She was disgusted. "What I don't know is why. Part of the reason I wanted to see you get another job was to get away from him, Beth. You're too good for him."

She'd said this many times before, and I hated hearing it. Part of me was comfortable, even glad, that Steve and I would still work at the same place.

"Those are the airplanes." I pointed to the Cubs to change the subject.

"Who flies those biplanes?"

"The Stearmans? Only the pilots who've been with him a few seasons and have a lot of experience. Brian said if I'm with him next year, he'll put me in one. They're a lot more airplane than the Cubs. Six hundred horse compared to the Cubs' one eighty."

We watched one of the Cubs taxi out. These were a later version of our own J-3 at Beverly. They had more power, wider fuselage, and wing flaps, along with other modifications. With the extra power Brian had added, they were off the ground before the throttle even went to full power. The one we were watching was a J-5, and in no time at all, it was in the air.

"So what happens now?" Melanie asked me.

The J-5 did a quick, tight pattern and came back around to the final leg. "The crew lays the banner on the grass to the right of the runway with its tow rope suspended between two poles, about six feet high. Now watch what he does: he's building up speed for the pickup, his tow line has a hook attached at the end. Now he's lining up between the poles..." We watched the pilot swoop between the poles stuck in the ground. "And he's got it." The Cub hooked the banner tow rope with its own hook and headed skyward for the critical climb, nose up, and the plane dramatically slowed by the drag it had just taken on. "I've learned that the pickup is the fun part, the part that gets the adrenaline going. The rest is routine. At the end of the tow, you fly back over the grass, pull the hook release inside the airplane, and it drops to the ground."

"Has Steve started yet?"

"Yes," I answered. "I think he's going out alone today." I did not want to talk about it. Once again, he had overstepped me.

Melanie looked at me. "You mean he's already checked out?"

"Uh huh."

"You know what the difference is between you and Steve?" she asked, not expecting an answer from me.

"Yeah, I know the difference," I said. "Steve's got more experience. What gets me is the fact that I'll never catch up with him."

"Wrong!" Melanie practically shouted. "We're talking about flying airplanes here, not rocket science. The difference between you two is he has more confidence than you, not necessarily skill."

I shrugged my shoulders. Melanie saw my reaction and knew to drop the subject.

"This weekend," I said, "Brian will give me my first official tows if the training finishes up as planned."

Melanie nodded. We turned our faces to the sun and our attention to the planes in the pattern. It was a busy afternoon at Lawrence, a sure sign of the coming summer season.

"I hope you'll still have time to fly with me in our own Cub," she asked.

"Of course."

We both smiled, faces still turned toward the sun.

CHAPTER 12

Scorpion Bowls

Steve sipped through one straw and I sipped through another on the Scorpion Bowl that sat between us. It was the signature drink at Chinaland Restaurant. The level in the bowl went down slowly, and before it was even half gone, I had a pleasant buzz.

"Don't suck it all down before you get any food in your stomach. I don't want to have to carry you home," Steve said.

Chinaland was Steve's favorite restaurant. For him, Chinese food didn't get better than what they served. My experience with Chinese food in China bore no similarity to the pupu platter he ordered, or anything else on Chinaland's menu. But it was Beverly's best, and we ate there often.

"You're still shaking, aren't you?" he asked and took my hand.

I nodded, appreciating the rare act of compassion.

He let go of my hand. "Are you going to go right back up tomorrow?"

"I don't know. I don't really know if I want to do any more banner-towing. I've had my thrills with it for a couple months now, but maybe it's time to look for something else. Towing banners requires more physical strength than I have." I hated myself for admitting it, but it had become obvious.

"What happened today had nothing at all to do with strength. And besides, it's not so much the banners that are hard to tow, it's the huge billboards," he said. Billboards were a new arrival to the business of banner-towing. Instead of stringing letters together to create a message, a billboard was a huge solid sheet of fabric painted with a brand or logo and was four or five times the size, weight, and drag of a banner.

"Do you remember two weeks ago when I had the bank billboard for a three-hour tow?"

"Uh huh."

"Well, there wasn't enough elevator trim on the plane to hold the nose up with that enormous thing hanging off the tail. The strength I needed to keep the stick back was unbelievable. No, it wasn't unbelievable, it was miserable. For two hours, I held the stick back with one leg crossed over the mother leg, and I had to keep switching from leg to leg because I got so tired."

Steve laughed, almost mockingly.

"It's not funny at all," I rebuked him. "I can't believe I'd tell you something like that, and you'd laugh."

"Whatever." He shrugged his shoulders. I went back to the scorpion bowl for some comfort. The pupu platter arrived. "You want to split another scorpion bowl?" he asked.

I nodded and returned to my straw. I always paid half the bill, so polite hesitation played no part when we were together.

My thoughts mellowed, and the day's events seemed as if from a dream. It was only when I looked down at my bandaged hand that I remembered it wasn't a dream. It started as my day off, but when I went to the office to pick up my paycheck, Brian asked if I would fly the new Gold Bond foot power billboard so one of the company executives could preview it. Just once around the traffic pattern so he could see it in the air. I pre-flighted Cub

Number 3 while the ground crew set the billboard up for the pickup. It was the biggest billboard yet, just recently completed in gold, red, and black. It would look like a giant canister of foot powder in the sky.

I took off, made the pickup on the first go-around, flew one rectangular pattern around the airport for good viewing, and got clearance from the tower to drop the billboard on my next pass. It was an easy extra few dollars in my next paycheck, always needed. When I pulled on the cable to release it on the grass, though, I did not hear or feel the familiar pop of the cable as the hook released its burden.

"Tower, Two-Nine-Papa requesting another go-around. The banner didn't release," I requested.

"Roger, Two-Nine-Papa, cleared for the go-around." No one else was in the pattern.

I probably didn't pull hard enough on the cable. But on the second try, and the third, and the fourth, I still had no success. I got on the company frequency with Brian, who was watching from the side of the runway.

"Yeah, Beth, what's the problem?" he asked calmly.

"I'm pulling the release as hard as I can," I answered, "but the hook won't give."

"Give it another try," Brian instructed.

The tower cleared me for a fifth pass, and I yanked with all my strength on the taut metal cable. Still no success.

"Try again," came the instructions for a sixth pass.

Exasperated from throwing all my weight into pulling that cable, I began to plan in my head a landing with the billboard attached. They had trained me on the technique of landing with a banner that did not release, but we never discussed a billboard landing, and I could now see why. It would demolish the airplane and probably the pilot, too. The billboard was so tall that it would hit the runway long before the airplane could touch down, and the sudden drag would bring the plane down violently. But what other choice would I have if I couldn't shed this monster on my tail?

By the sixth pass, the cable was red and sticky with blood from my hand. I used both hands to pull, temporarily surrendering control of the plane. The billboard still did not release.

"Dammit!" I tried not to think about Brian's previous lost pilots.

"Beth," Brian's voice called me. "Listen carefully. I have a plan. I want you to fly out over the marsh by Plum Island and wait there for me at one thousand feet. I'm going to take the Stearman and meet you there. I want to try to come up from behind you and cut the billboard cable with my prop. I don't know if it'll work, but we've got to try. There's obviously a problem with your hook mechanism."

The flight to the marsh seemed to take forever. Airspeed with the enormous billboard was less than I'd flown in any other airplane. It gave me plenty of time to think about the predicament. What if he couldn't cut the line? What if I had to land with this thing still hitched? Even worse, what if he got tangled up in the billboard as he did in the accident Rod told me about? Then we'd both be going down. I went over each possible scenario as I circled the marsh at the assigned altitude, waiting for Brian.

"Do you see where I am, Beth?" Brian asked over the company frequency.

I did a ninety-degree turn and spotted him. "Yes, I see you."

"Okay," he said, "take a heading of zero-nine-zero and go into slow flight. Let me know when you're established."

Slow flight? What did he think I was doing now? Still, I took it back as far as possible without stalling. A minute later, I gave him the okay.

"Now, hold it as steady as you can, constant speed, constant heading. I'm gonna line up behind you at a slight angle and a little below you. If it looks like I can pull it off, I'll get close enough for the prop to cut the line. Remember, hold steady—constant speed, constant heading."

There was a nervousness in his own voice now I hadn't heard before. With this maneuver, he was taking the chance of getting his propeller tangled up with the line instead of just cutting the line. It had to be perfectly executed. My body was tense. I held Cub Number Three as steady as possible, watching airspeed and heading as if waiting for a time bomb to explode. I could hear him coming up behind me as the seconds passed like hours.

Then, as though nothing at all, there was a jolt of my plane, and it lurched forward as the drag was eliminated from its tail. The giant foot powder billboard fell to the marsh below.

"Okay," Brian declared, his voice lightened, "you're all set. Let's go back to Lawrence."

I followed the Stearman back and landed after Brian did. A very concerned crew was waiting along with some pilots, including Steve. He looked mildly concerned.

I pulled in front of the tie-down spot, took a deep breath, shut the engine down, and climbed out. Brian met me halfway across the ramp before we reached the others. He looked at me seriously and said, "If some of the others tell you you're lucky to be alive, I want you to know what they're talking about. On your last pass, the billboard cleared the trees at the end of the runway by only a few feet. It was this far away from catching the trees," he showed me with his hands, "and if it had, you would have gone in. I lost a pilot that way three years ago."

His words bit through me, and I looked at the trees.

"You did great." He put his arm around my shoulders. "Let's get a bandage on that hand."

———

The pupu platter and the second scorpion bowl were all I needed, but now there were three more dishes on the table. I picked out the water chestnuts, baby corn, and mushrooms with my chopsticks, leaving the rest for Steve.

"I've given Brian two weeks' notice," he told me. "I wanted to have some fun with the banners, but there's another opportunity that will get me the multi-engine hours I want."

"What opportunity?"

"Before I went to Brian's today," he explained, "I went over to the other side of Lawrence Airport and applied for a job. I'll be flying freight for a new charter outfit over there called Cash Air."

I didn't know what to say. I knew I didn't want to tow banners anymore, but was I qualified to fly charters?

He continued, "This is the step I've been waiting for. Twin-engine freight charter. The guy who owns the company— Reynald Ouellette—"

I raised my eyebrows.

"He's French Canadian. They call him Ren for short. Anyway, he's got seven planes. Five Navajo Chieftains, a regular Navajo, a Seneca, and an Archer. I'll mainly be flying the Chieftains, late-night flying. Ren has a couple nightly routes through Teterboro, New Jersey, one out of Buffalo, and another through Boston and Burlington, Vermont. And in two weeks, he'll be starting two big multi-city routes in the Midwest based out of Chicago Midway." He paused and took another long drink of the scorpion bowl. "There's good flying at Cash Air," he continued. "It's going to be my ticket to the airlines."

He was getting further away from me with every sentence.

"His Chief Pilot is starting the next ground class soon. The flights are operated under Part 135 of the regs,[8] so they have to do ground training and a check ride with the pilots to meet the regs."

I sat still in my seat. "Will you have to move?"

"Maybe."

The irony was painfully obvious. Where he had preceded me at New England Flyers, I preceded him towing banners for Brian. Now it was his turn to take the next step ahead of me. Like a simple board game, we were taking turns moving past each other, except that I knew I could never leave him too far behind. He still had the advantage of many more flight hours.

"Is he still hiring?" I asked, already planning my next step.

"Yeah, I think so." He shoveled a forkful of Kung Pao chicken into his mouth. "Call him and see."

---

8   Part 135 is a section of the Federal Aviation Regulations that governs "the carriage in air commerce of persons or property for compensation or hire as a commercial operator (not an air carrier) in aircraft having a maximum seating capacity of less than 20 passengers or a maximum payload capacity of less than 6,000 pounds." [FAR Part 135.1, Applicability]

CHAPTER 13

Cash Air

On the last night of May, the sound of heavy rain woke me during the early morning hours. By the time my alarm went off an hour later, the rain had stopped, leaving only a thick cloud cover. I was up early to get ready for ground training at Cash Air. Even though had far fewer hours than Steve, the chief pilot hired me on the spot.

I spent the week before reading Part 135 of the Federal Aviation Regulations, tedious with its detailed rules on weather, training, time, and equipment. I also studied the Piper Navajo operation manual to learn its speeds and limits, systems, and performance. The transition would require confidence, both in knowledge of the material and handling of the aircraft. The first days of ground training would cover the book material, and I was confident with that. But soon I would have to perform in the airplane, possibly alongside Steve.

I looked out the bedroom window at the wet street. In my mind, I attempted to construct an initial training flight in the Navajo from the pre-flight inspection to startup and taxi for takeoff to landing and shutdown. I based my thoughts on the few minutes I had spent in the Navajo cockpit just the day before at Cash Air, along with what I had learned from the aircraft manual. The airplane had more power and instruments than anything I had flown so far. This was a huge step.

As the morning commute came to life outside the window, I was landing the Navajo in my virtual training session. Convinced I had done all I could to prepare for the day, I retreated from my thoughts to the warm shower.

———

Steve and I arrived at Lawrence Airport at the same time, on the other side of the field from Brian Patterson's banner-towing operation. He gave me a quick kiss in the parking lot before we climbed the long set of stairs to Cash Air's space above the airport's newest hangar. There were several rooms on the second floor, one with a large window overlooking the tarmac in front of the hangar. They had set up a classroom for six people in the first room, and the smell of coffee and a box of doughnuts greeted us. Four others were there already. The last two seats were ours.

"You're Beth and Steve," said a voice across the room. "Am I right?"

"I hope so," Steve answered.

"I'm Ken Ahern," the same voice told us. Ken's face was gentle, with sparse blonde curls barely covering his head. I had heard Ren say a few days earlier that he was on the rebound from chemotherapy. The cancer was in remission, but Ken still showed the signs of a body recovering. He introduced the others. "This is Peter Covich, Danny McLaughlin, and Drew Petrucci. I'll be doing your training in the Navajo."

"Are you two related?" the one named Peter asked Steve and me. Danny and Drew were looking at us without a word, perhaps sizing up what our flight experience might be. Peter didn't seem to care about those differences. A handsome innocence came across in his smile and words.

"No. No, we're not," I answered, surprised by the question as always. Steve and I had heard the question several times before. Our hair was the same dark brown, thick and straight, and we both had brown eyes, but the similarities went no further than that, and our personalities were completely different.

"Have all of you been checked out to fly yet?" I asked.

"I guess you could say that," Peter replied. "I've been flying the Seneca. Not the Navajos. But the Seneca's fine with me. I'm the only one who flies it, and let's face it, multi-engine time is multi-engine time in the logbook."

I nodded in acknowledgement, thinking of my own totals to date. I had only logged a little over seven hundred hours, several hundred short of being legal for this job. Peter appeared no older than twenty-one or twenty-two and probably had logged about five hundred hours. But Ren didn't seem to care, so it was our express ticket to the airlines. We were all well aware that accumulating flight hours was the key to being hired by the airlines.

"Isn't the ground training supposed to happen before you get checked out in the airplane?" I asked.

"Technically, yes," Ken answered. "But in the Cash Air world, the ground training happens when you read the aircraft manual and you're sitting in the airplane with the instructor. What you get out of today doesn't have much to do with the success of a flight."

"Good morning, y'all. Where's the doughnuts?" Harry Pace walked into the classroom, his gut preceding him through the doorway. Cash Air's Chief Pilot, he was a middle-aged

Missourian and a former Army pilot. He looked a little like Ren, even acted like him. The only difference between them was their flying backgrounds. Both began about the same time in the nineteen sixties, but Ren was a civil aviation pilot.

"Well, then," Harry began, "I guess we have to cover a few things these couple of days to keep the Feds happy." He bit into a jelly doughnut, and red jelly oozed out of the other end. "But before we go knee deep into that crap, let's talk about what you folks really want to hear about and what I love to talk about—money and airplanes."

With powdered sugar stuck under his nose and on his chin, Harry spent the next hour explaining how we would be paid. When it came time for the discussion of regulations, his interest departed, and he assumed the same for us. The morning went slowly until Ren came to the door at about eleven o'clock.

"What the hell's on your face, Pace?" Ren interrupted the monologue on weather requirements.

"What?" Harry asked, suddenly paranoid. He dragged the back of his hand across his mouth. "What?"

Ren ignored him. "Who wants to take a flight down to New Bedford? How about you, Puchalski?"

"Sure, what's up?" Steve was always ready to fire up an airplane for any reason. Nothing else came before that.

"All you gotta do is take a box down there. It has a hazmat sticker on it, but don't worry, it's not radioactive. Somebody'll meet you there to pick it up."

Ren had a whiney voice with a little smile that somehow made it funny. It was never not that way. I looked at him now and bit my lip to keep from laughing at the short, round man in the doorway who ran things around here.

Harry looked irritated, his face now free of the powdered sugar. "What're you doing? I'm trying to conduct a ground school here and keep everything legal."

"Look, fat boy," Ren came back, "I'm trying to run a charter company and keep these young people employed. If you think the hogshit the FAA tells us to preach to them is more important than getting out there and making dollars, then you're even dumber than you told me you were." His eyes glowed, and it was plain that neither of them took each other too seriously. Except for the dollars.

He walked away, still smirking, and Steve followed him.

"This is a great start," Ken said after they left. "Steve has no check ride, no hazmat training, and Ren's sending him out on a flight with hazardous materials in an airplane that's not even on our certificate and isn't IFR-certified for Part 135." He shook his head. "I will pretend I didn't see that."

"You've been in Buffalo for the past week, right?" Harry asked smoothly.

"Yeah…"

"Then you're real tired."

"Yeah, Harry, you're right," said Ken, "which makes it that much more difficult to remember."

Harry patted Ken on the back. "That's right, buddy, this is the real world of flying, not the one the Feds try to make us live in."

The hours in front of the chalkboard passed slowly. In the late afternoon, Steve walked back in, his clothes wet from the misty air outside. He had the cockiness of a mission successfully completed, and he was the star pilot who had done it.

"Low IFR?" I asked him.

He shrugged. "Not bad."

"First 135 flight, Puchalski? How'd it go?" Harry asked.

"A lot better having a box to keep you company than some pain-in-the-ass student," Steve laughed. In fact, everyone laughed except me. I had been his student. He leaned back in his seat, legs stretched out in front of him, arms folded across his chest.

"There will be a lot more than just one box to keep you company on the real runs," Harry informed him. "You'll be bulging at the sides with newspapers. Ken and Peter already know about that."

"Yeah, that Seneca's coming apart at the seams with the loads they've been giving me," Peter said. "The original loading has gone up by a few hundred pounds since the route started. Friday night I had seven hundred fifty pounds out of Teterboro. That took some juggling on my weight and balance."

Harry rubbed his chin. "Well, that route will eventually need a Navajo. That's what they're paying for anyway. But there's a better profit on the Seneca, so if we can squeeze it all in, let's keep doing it."

"Are you still spewing useless knowledge to these people?" Ren stood in the doorway again.

"We're done now. How about a few beers?" Harry spoke to no one in particular.

"I don't think so," replied Ken. "I've got to head back out to Buffalo in the morning for the week. Kind of like to spend some time with my wife."

"Puchalski, you're ready for a check ride," Harry announced. "We can do that in the morning, and then you can go to Buffalo for this week, maybe next week, too. Let Ken spend time with his wife. After that, I want you in Chicago when those runs start."

"Sounds good." Steve was satisfied.

"And Beth," Harry continued, "I think I'll have you fly with Ken this week for some training on the Teterboro run. Peter, you can stay on call here with the Seneca."

"Yes, sir!"

"Alright, that's settled." Harry rubbed his hands together. "Steve's going to Buffalo tomorrow, Ken can have a few beers with us, and the company is operating like a well-oiled machine."

Ren laughed and walked back down the hallway.

———

I was sure I knew the answer, but I asked anyway. "You want to come over tonight?" And then, before Steve could answer, "You'll be gone for a week or two."

"I've got to get my stuff together for the morning, but my father's not around, so you can come over to my house," he proposed.

I agreed, though a night at Steve's house meant little sleep sharing a single bed.

"Let's get going," he said. "I want to get to sleep early."

I asked myself why I was going as I followed him to the parking lot. Each step took me further away from my dignity. I was growing to recognize and hate my dependence on him for approval and self-esteem. It had been obvious for a while now that Steve provided neither. My brain tried in vain to console my heart with the idea that a week or two apart from him would be time to strengthen, perhaps grow away, but my heart rejected the cold consolation. No matter how I looked at it, I still felt the need to hang on.

Steve packed his clothes as I watched from where I sat on his tall bed. It was as tall as the mattress was wide, and though it was unclear why it was so tall, I wrote it off as just one more peculiar part of the house. Had he ever fallen out as a child, and if so, had he cried? Had he ever cried in his life? I couldn't imagine so.

"Jerry's going to jail," he said, folding a shirt.

"What?" His words broke into my thoughts.

"Jerry Kennedy—he was convicted, he's going to jail."

"What happened?"

"The Feds found empty bottles inside the airplane, and you already know his alcohol level was way up there." He folded another shirt.

"So what did they charge him with?"

"Two counts of voluntary manslaughter."

"Oh, God. He'll be in jail for a long time."

"Yeah, but he's got Harriet out there working on his appeal with the lawyer."

"He's got to live with the guilt of having caused those deaths for the rest of his life. And what does Harriet have to do with it, anyway?"

"They've been going out since last winter," he informed me. "You didn't know?"

"Sounds like she needs a purpose in her life, and Jerry's now that purpose." I didn't hide my contempt.

"Whatever you think of her, Harriet is a very nice person," Steve defended her.

I rolled my eyes. "I'll never know what you saw in that woman. For God's sake, she's twelve years older than you and prematurely gray." I hoped he would agree, or at least recognize what I said, but he gave me the apathetic look I hated, shrugged, and walked by me to the closet.

Several minutes passed, and I watched his oddly meticulous method of sorting and packing. Remembering he would be away these next few weeks, I tried to look past his peculiar ways.

"I'll miss you," I said. It was a futile attempt to feel a closeness with him.

"Aww, it's not for that long." He tossed me half a smile and returned to his T-shirts.

"Do you think Harry will send me out to Chicago, too?"

"I don't know. Ask him."

"I assumed we'd both be sent out there when the Chicago routes started. He'll probably send me after I get my check ride."

"I told you, Beth, I don't know. Why don't you just ask him?"

I dropped the subject. Several minutes passed in silence, and he collected some things from the bathroom down the hall.

"Have you heard from Adam?" I asked when he returned.

"No, but I was at Beverly the other day and saw him doing touch-and-gos in one of Rod's Cherokees."

"He's starting from scratch?"

"That's right. They revoked his license, which means you start over as if you'd never flown before."

I sighed. "That's a tough deal, but he's lucky he didn't get himself killed in that whole mess. Those are two stellar examples of drinking and flying. Jerry and Adam." It made me feel better knowing I never combined drinking and flying, but I was fooling myself thinking drinking and flying was the only combination that could end a pilot's career, let alone their life.

Steve put his bag on the floor and asked, "You about ready to go to sleep? I'm tired and want to get a good night's rest for tomorrow."

Ten minutes later, he was sound asleep next to me in the single bed; I lay facing the window with little hope for the same. The clouds of the day had cleared, and an almost full moon shed light in the little room. I followed the light to a corner of the ceiling and traced its outline above me. It was an oddly shaped room made up of six sides and five angles. There seemed to be no reason for the random jogs the walls took to create the space.

I looked at the only window in the room and focused on the fragment of moon it revealed. For the foreseeable future, I would fly in this same night sky, except that the benefit of moonlight might not be available, more likely obscured by clouds and thunderstorms. I had little experience flying at night since my night hours totaled less than a hundred, but soon I'd have my check ride and the responsibility of transporting newspapers at night, alone in a twin-engine aircraft, hopefully confident in my abilities.

CHAPTER 14

First Night

"You have the credit card?" Harry asked.

"Got it," I answered.

"And some cash?"

"Yup."

"You know the route instructions?"

"Buffalo, Jamestown, Rochester, Teterboro, Buffalo. Pick up checks in Jamestown and then Rochester, bring them back to Teterboro. Pick up the newspapers in Teterboro, bring them to Buffalo," I recited. "Except for today because it's Sunday. No checks, so I go straight to Teterboro."

"And you know the name of the hotel where you're staying?"

"The Airways Hotel, right on the airport."

"Okay, honey, I guess you're all set," Harry declared. "You did fine in the airplane. Here's your paperwork in case the Feds come strolling across the ramp with their eyes on you. And don't you be scared of that Navajo Chieftain. It's no different from the regular Navajo we just flew. Just the engines are bigger, the props counter-rotate, and you get a couple extra feet of airplane and a door by the pilot seat. You know all that."

It had been a tough week. For the first couple of days, I was missing having Steve around—or rather my needy subconscious was missing Steve. It affected my learning curve on the Navajo. Not only that, but I had to make the switch from a day schedule to the night freight schedule, so I didn't get much sleep. I had to learn the route, air traffic control details, the paperwork and, of course, how to fly the airplane. By the end of the week, Ken told Harry and Ren that I was ready for my check ride. One more pilot for the line.

Harry continued, "You answered all my questions with no problem. Most important thing is you get the job done and have a good time doing it. Any other questions?"

"No, that's it." I wanted him to leave.

He patted me on the back and turned to the airplane we had flown from Beverly to Buffalo. "See ya, hon. We'll be thinking of you in Chicago," he said over his shoulder.

"See ya."

Carrying my flight bag and an overnight case stuffed with enough clothes for the week, I turned back to the airplane I would be flying. November Niner-Two-Two-Alpha-Charlie— N922AC—a Navajo Chieftain. Harry told me I wouldn't have a problem transitioning from the regular Navajo they trained me in to this slightly larger and more powerful version of the same plane. He had given me what they call "differences training" as required by the regs, and I had flown copilot in another Chieftain once with Ken. Harry said it was enough to get the idea.

I dropped my bags on the ground and climbed onto the left wing, unlatched the pilot's door and stepped in. The airplane was hot from sitting in the sun on the black tarmac, and I immediately walked to the rear to open the passenger door for ventilation. The top half of the door opened slowly on its hydraulic control while the bottom half—with the stairs attached—dropped with a thud. I sat in the open doorway and watched the other freight planes scattered on the ramp.

Already tired from a long, hot day, my mind wandered. I thought about the training method and the check ride Harry gave me and wondered how typical it was for these Part 135 freight companies. It had been a strange ride out here to Buffalo with Harry. He called it my check ride, but it was unlike any other check ride I'd had. We flew from Lawrence to Buffalo, did an instrument approach in under clear skies, and landed. There were no maneuvers required, no stalls, no engine-out approach, not even an engine-out in flight. Instead, he asked me to recite the engine-out checklist while we were on our way. My training with Ken had involved little practice with engine-out procedures, just two or three times, but if an engine-out ever became a reality, I had the checklist memorized, and hopefully that would be good enough. Or would it?

I looked to the other side of the ramp as a DC-4, one of Steve's favorite vintage planes, fired up. He and I had spoken just twice, briefly, since he left for Chicago. I would not see him for at least another week. Cash Air's planning progressed only one week at a time, and for the foreseeable future, it was Buffalo for me.

I walked to the front of the airplane. The clipboard was on the copilot's seat with a full supply of blank weight and balance forms along with others for flight times, mechanical problems, etc. I ran my eyes over the instrument panel to familiarize myself with Two-Alpha-Charlie and noticed it included three-color weather radar. If it was working, it would be a support in the summer thunderstorms ahead. Aside from the radios and the engines, the only thing a Cash Air pilot could count on being functional was the very expensive Northstar Loran that Ren had installed in each of the Navajos. As long as there were

VFR flight conditions, the Northstar allowed navigation entirely by its guidance, whether the destination was Buffalo or San Francisco. Maybe having it compensated for any other broken equipment, at least in Ren's mind.

———

The Airways Hotel was old, probably built when commercial flights began servicing Buffalo. It would be livable as long as my room was not under a takeoff or approach path.

It had been a long day with Harry and a long week with Ken. I put my bags on one bed and dropped onto the other. The clock on the nightstand read four o'clock. Departure time for the run was seven o'clock because there was no freight going out of Buffalo on Sundays. I would fly empty on the first leg.

I closed my eyes and when I opened them again, it was five thirty. Time to call Flight Service. The person on the other end of the line told me the conditions were clear the whole way. Everything looked smooth until the time came to leave Teterboro. They predicted thunderstorms unless they fizzled out in the meantime, but that was not likely, the briefer told me. Plan for some thunderstorms.

The sleep refreshed me, and it did not matter that I would not see the bed again until after two in the morning. I was ready for my first flight under FAR Part 135, my first flight alone in any multi-engine plane, and my first night flight alone. Maybe even my first flight through a thunderstorm. With a chocolate bar for energy and my flight bag packed, I closed the door behind me, walked down the dark hall to the front desk, and requested a ride to the freight terminal. They saw the routine week after week with Cash Air pilots.

A middle-aged woman looked up from her newspaper. "Fred's in the car, same car he picked you up in. Right out front," she told me as she pointed to the brown station wagon.

I opened the door and slid into the front seat, throwing my flight bag into the back. "Hi, Fred."

"Hey," he greeted me with a smile and a cigarette between his lips. "How're you doin'? You get some sleep?" He started the car.

"Enough to get me through the night, I hope."

"Good job. But it's only Monday. The other guys are always real tired by the end of the week. Except that one guy last week. Steve. You know him?" Fred asked.

"Yeah, I know him."

"What a hot shit he is. Full of energy the whole week. He seems to thrive on flyin', like it's all he lives for." Fred pressed his cigarette out in the ashtray. "Give him a little food and water, a little sleep, and fill in the rest with flying. You notice that about him?"

"Oh, yeah. For him, nothing comes before flying." *Not me, not his family, not nothing,* I thought to myself.

"Actually kind of a weird dude if you think about it."

He pulled up in front of the freight terminal. I stepped out and opened the back door to get my bag.

"Thanks, Fred," I said through the open window. "Do you work the night shift?"

"Double shifts all the time, so I'll be pickin' you up when you get in. Just call."

I walked through a metal building that was part of the freight terminal to get to the ramp on the other side. Two-Alpha-Charlie sat alone in a far corner of the general aviation ramp, close to the trailers that housed offices for the freight agents. I had no business with them today, not until tomorrow when they would have bags of cancelled checks for me to take to Jamestown and Rochester.

The ramp still radiated the heat of the day's sun, but it was more tolerable now. I opened the aircraft doors and proceeded to pre-flight the exterior, carefully checking this airplane I had never flown before.

It was an oddly configured plane that Ren bought at auction. Originally purchased new from the Piper factory by a small, ill-fated company in Maine, it later found itself in the owner-ship of a Mexican drug runner who outfitted it with extra fuel tanks. Normal configuration for a Navajo Chieftain was four fuel cells—two in each wing, one inboard and one outboard—but Two-Alpha-Charlie had two additional tanks in each of the engine nacelles, the housings that covered the engines. Before coming to Cash Air, it had also had a large tank in the fuselage itself, giving it a very long range. The huge fuselage tank had been removed, but the nacelle tanks were still in place, and I would learn that they could be very useful.

The normal procedure for the Buffalo to Teterboro run was to fill only the four original wing tanks upon arrival back in Buffalo at night. Fuel was cheaper in Buffalo than Teterboro, and Ren preferred we take on enough to avoid the extra costs of buying it in when we stopped in Teterboro even though that was what all the other pilots did. I checked and found that the cells were full after Steve's last flight, the nacelles were empty, and everything else checked out fine as I walked around.

I laid my charts and clipboard on the copilot's seat. Because Steve would never file a flight plan unless conditions were strictly IFR, I decided not to file either. VFR the whole way: VFR charts and the Northstar Loran for guidance. Confident that the aircraft was ready, I reached up and flipped the master switch. The electrical system began humming, and I pushed the starter switch for the left engine. It turned over quickly, and I pulled the throttle back to idle and started the right engine.

By the time I had taxied to the end of Runway 14, I was ready for this flight. I had given it so much thought in advance and felt I had already flown it a thousand times before. When the tower cleared me for takeoff, I pulled the pilot door shut and latched it. I brought the power up slowly and evenly until the turbochargers kicked in, accelerating down the runway centerline.

Alpha-Charlie was light with no cargo and jumped into the air. I turned on course for a straight line to Teterboro, the Loran as my guidance, and climbed to three thousand feet. I focused my attention on the gauges, shifting from that to scan the surrounding sky for other traffic.

I was just ten minutes into the flight when I began hearing a hissing sound. The source was over my shoulder, coming from the pilot's door. I had latched it before takeoff, so I didn't understand what could be wrong. My eyes and ears followed the latch at the base of the door all the way around the door's seal up to the top. Another latch. A bigger, more important latch, and it was undone.

Simple enough, I said to myself. *Grab the door handle to pull it in.* I reached for the upper latch, but it was impossible to overcome the force of the air that was swelling the door. I could not close the tiny distance between the latch and its catch at the top of the door. For a moment, I left it alone and tried to ignore the sound. But it persisted, hissing in my ear. The door swelled even more now that I established the airplane at a cruise speed of 165 knots. I cursed the door and the airplane and Harry and Ren as I tried again to latch the top.

I threw up my arms in defeat and took a long, deep breath. And another. Landing was not an option, it would make me late. It occurred to me that I should just slow the plane down and start from the beginning—unlatch the door and refasten it. I pulled back the throttles and props and established the airspeed at about 130 knots. Without a second thought, I grabbed the door handle with my left hand and unlatched the bottom with my right. The moment those forces that had been swelling the door had the vaguest notion they were about to win the fight, the door flew open and out of my control. I grabbed the handle and pulled as hard as I could, my other hand ready for the top latch. But as I should have known from the start, my strength had no chance of matching the force between me and the door. And as if to reinforce that fact, the door began banging against the airplane as soon as I let go.

Bang! Bang! Bang!

It was loud, constant, and unstoppable. I tried again to close the door without success. Frustrated and now just plain scared, I had to fly this thing—*bang bang bang*—another 225 miles to Teterboro. The heat seemed to build in the cockpit—*bang bang bang*—and sweat formed on my forehead and neck. To land and correct the situation was my only choice. I pulled the chart from the copilot's seat and—*bang bang bang*—scanned it for the closest airport. There was an uncontrolled field, Dansville Municipal, with 3,500 feet of runway about 20 miles away. According to the Loran, 18.3 miles, with a heading of 117 degrees. I turned to the course—*bang bang bang*—and began a slow descent.

Dansville came quickly into sight, and I said a short prayer of thanks for that. I positioned myself to land straight in on Runway 14. I needed to get the damned plane—*bang bang bang*—on the ground.

"Dansville Unicom, Navajo Niner-Two-Two-Alpha-Charlie is four miles out," I announced, "making a straight in approach to Runway 14. Any traffic, please advise."

My hands were shaking and my mind distracted—*bang bang bang*—as I spoke, but no one responded, and it seemed I was alone at Dansville. I turned to final at one mile out. As I sped to the runway at too high a speed, coming in high and fast over the runway numbers—*bang bang bang*—I saw half of the runway disappear behind me.

"Damn it! You son of a bitch!" I put the power back in and aborted the landing. "Dansville Unicom, Two-Alpha-Charlie going around, left traffic for Runway 14," I blurted out.

I turned to the final leg again as the sun dropped into the trees west of the airport.

"Dansville, Two-Alpha-Charlie,"—*bang bang bang*—"turning final on one four."

It was a short final, too short, and though this time my airspeed was where it should be, I hadn't put the flaps down. Once again, I soared high and fast over the numbers. Another go-around. I poured in the power and swore even louder. *Bang bang bang*. I was embarrassed and angry at myself. *Don't let the airplane fly you, you fly the airplane.* Over and over, I said it to myself, almost hearing Steve's voice.

I did not announce myself on the radio this third time around but gave special attention to flying a larger pattern with plenty of time to prepare. When I turned to the final leg, my gear was down prematurely—*bang bang bang*—and flaps and airspeed not yet under control. On short final, I extended the flaps to forty degrees, fully down, and airspeed at a barely acceptable 120 knots. The plane touched down, and though the banging had stopped, it still resounded in my head.

I turned off at the end and taxied to the ramp. With the engines shut down, I climbed out through the door that had been taunting me. The ramp was empty, just one Cessna on the grass by a hangar painted barn red. There was a small office attached to the hangar, also painted barn red, and the door was open. The screen door slammed behind me as I entered, and a mechanic appeared from the hangar when he heard it. It seemed he was alone.

"Looked like you were havin' some trouble out there. Saw you go around a couple times," he said plainly, but with enough curiosity to hope for an explanation.

"Yeah, I was having a problem with the flaps." I tossed the words off quickly and turned to find the bathroom.

I sat on the toilet and put my head in my hands. My body was still trembling. *Pull yourself together now, Beth. There's no time for this, you have a job to do.* I splashed cold water on my face and dried it.

"You got your problem worked out now?" the mechanic asked when I emerged from the bathroom. I couldn't tell if he believed the story of the flaps.

"All set, thanks for asking."

By the time the screen door slammed behind me the second time, daylight had faded. The air was calm and the sky clear. Alpha-Charlie waited on the ramp, pilot door wide open as if mocking me. I climbed onto the left wing and slid through the opening and back into my seat.

While taxiing to the runway, I checked that none of the circuit breakers had popped, flaps went down okay, trim set, oil and fuel pressure in the green. It was the abbreviated Cash Air takeoff checklist. My own final preparation for takeoff this time, though, included a rigorous check of the questionable door, opening and closing and locking it three, maybe four times.

I taxied into position and gave the door one more visual check before starting the takeoff roll. Confident I was now ready to get myself to Teterboro, I brought the power up. As I accelerated down the runway, I felt something holding the airplane back, some kind of resistance. My eyes darted around the instrument panel looking for a clue. Everything checked normal until I glanced at the right wing. The flaps were down in the full forty-degree position. I quickly looked back to the flap controller and then to the indicator, both to the right of the throttle quadrant. They showed normal. I yanked the throttles back to abort the takeoff.

Back on the taxiway again, I shook my head with frustration and wondered if I was being cursed with the very problem I had lied about to the mechanic. My efforts to either raise the flaps back to the up position or come up with an answer to the problem failed.

"You're back?" the mechanic asked when I walked through the door again.

"It's the flaps...again. They're stuck down," I explained.

"You want me to take a look at it?" he offered.

I nodded. With a flashlight from the hangar, we walked out to the airplane. He went into the cockpit, and I followed. Then he went outside to the left wing, and I followed.

"It's probably the actuator," he finally said.

"Can you fix it?"

"Well, I know I can get your flaps back up, but that's where they'll stay until you replace the part. That's a special order item for most anyone."

I let out a sigh. "Can I use your phone?"

"Right inside on the desk. I'll work on getting these flaps back up."

I dreaded having to call Ren with the bad news. How could I tell him my first day on the line had only progressed fifty miles before the problems started? Steve had flown this route in this same airplane for a week without a problem.

"Ren?" I said when he answered. The phone rang at his home when the office was closed.

"Yeah."

"It's Beth. There's a problem."

"What do you mean?" he asked curtly.

"I'm in Dansville, New York, about fifty miles out of Buffalo. I landed because the pilot door came open in flight. Anyway, I'm on the ground now, and the flaps are stuck down at forty-degrees."

"Oh, shit! Can't you get them back up?"

"There's a mechanic doing that right now, but he said the flap actuator is bad and needs to be replaced. Once the flaps are back up, that's where they stay until it's repaired."

"So what's the problem?"

"Well, I told you. Once they're back up, they stay up," I repeated. "The flaps aren't working."

"Haven't you ever done a no-flap landing?"

I could picture the look on his face, the same one I had seen that day in the classroom when he was talking to Harry. "Sure I have."

"So what's the problem?"

"What are you telling me, Ren?" I questioned him on the obvious illegality of what he was suggesting. When I wasn't carrying freight, flying the airplane was legal with broken flaps, but the minute I took on payload freight, I fell under the commercial aviation regulations of Part 135, and that meant it *all* had to be in working order.

"You know how to land without flaps. Get in the goddamned airplane and fly it to Teterboro!"

"And then what?"

"What do you mean 'and then what'?" He was shouting now. "Get back in it and fly to Buffalo. And tomorrow do the same thing all over again. And the next day, and the next day, until the end of the week when it can come back here to be fixed." His point was very clear. After a moment, he continued, this time not shouting, "Look, Beth, I'm not trying to be an asshole, but I've got a business to run. If we can't make our deadlines to pick up and deliver the freight, then the newspaper will find someone else who can. That's how this business works—on-time, dependable performance...no matter what."

"Okay. Hope I didn't ruin your night, Ren."

"It takes a lot more than that to ruin my night. Just go get the job done, okay?"

I hung up the phone. It was dark outside, and there was a long night of flying ahead. Even with all that had already happened, it had hardly begun.

CHAPTER 15

First Night, Still

It wasn't a lie when I told Ren I had done no-flap landings. It was part of the required training for my private license. But that was in a Cherokee, and this was a Navajo. Not that a no-flap landing required much skill, but I had barely learned to fly a Navajo, let alone a Chieftain.

I never considered saying no to Ren. He would probably fire me. I needed this job to get my multi-engine time. That part was too good to pass up. And I was determined to show Ren I could do the job as capably as Steve, or any other pilot. If I said no, I became the female pilot who didn't have the proverbial balls to saddle up and go.

I had almost two hours of flying time between Dansville and Teterboro to consider the landing without flaps ahead. The tower controllers cleared me to land close to eleven o'clock on one-mile final. Right away I knew I was already coming in too high and too fast again. Without the extra drag of forty degrees of flaps, I tried to correct the approach in a panic. I didn't allow myself to consider the option of aborting the landing and going around for another try as I had done twice in Dansville. Teterboro was a busy commercial airport with much faster, bigger equipment constantly flying in and out. I didn't dare screw up the synchronized air traffic flow by announcing a go-around for stupid reasons. This wasn't a small municipal airport with plenty of time to spare.

On short final, my speed was still too fast and altitude about three hundred feet. I wasn't even close to being able to put the plane down when I crossed the runway numbers. The runway was five thousand feet long, and I hoped that was enough length to salvage the landing.

By the time I put it on the ground, I had floated over three-quarters of the runway before finally plunking it down firmly. Pressure on the brakes slowed me enough to turn on the taxiway with a shred of dignity.

I took a very deep breath and slowly let it out as I waited for instructions from ground control. The landing wasn't pretty, but still I was relieved to have it done. Now I knew I could function at some level without flaps.

——

By day, Teterboro Airport was a home away from home for corporate pilots. Only twelve miles from midtown Manhattan, the airport welcomed Learjets and Cessna Citations that arrived with their important, or at least self-important, passengers. By night, it transformed into a meeting point for freight carriers and freight agents. As freight pilots, we enjoyed the advantage of the daytime corporate traffic we otherwise would not have had—a nicely carpeted, clean lounge with comfortable sofas and recliners, television, and fresh coffee. I had learned while flying with Ken the week before that the early bird to Teterboro gets the worm. Here, the freight pilot who got him or herself to Teterboro early in the evening was the early bird, and the comfy sofas and recliners were the worms. The late arriver, as I was this evening, would have to wait until the early birds' freight agents arrived with their payload. Only then would a seat be vacated, so I didn't hurry to go inside.

I parked the plane on the ramp and made my notes in the log by the light of a flashlight. The fuel gauges showed consumption was already coming from the inboard tanks—the main tanks—and the outboards had less than a quarter of a tank each. Steve had said one fill-up in Buffalo was sufficient for the night if it was VFR, even with the stops at Jamestown and Rochester. It had been VFR the whole week for him, so I knew it was accurate. With the possibility of thunderstorms I might have to dodge during the flight back to Buffalo, extra fuel would be comforting. But the words of Ren, Harry, and Ken came back to me. "Don't buy fuel in Teterboro," they had said. "It's too expensive." Recalling Ren's tirade just a few hours earlier, I dismissed the option. If necessary, I could land on the way to Buffalo to put on a few extra gallons where it might be cheaper.

"You from Cash Air?" an agent asked as I walked across the ramp.

"Yes."

"About time you got here. I've got your load. Make sure you get here earlier from now on so you're ready to go," he scolded me. "I can see why they hired a skinny thing like you. More room for freight."

He was a cocky bastard with the attitude I'd been seeing a lot the week before. As near as I could tell, the non-pilots were in a position to give orders and instructions to the pilots, and they liked it. Maybe the fact that he was dealing with a woman pilot irritated him. Ken had warned me about this, so it wasn't a surprise, but it did make me wonder if the aviation world grew meaner with each step up the ladder.

I opened the cargo door while he drove his van through the gate. The ramp was cluttered with twin-engine propeller planes like Alpha-Charlie. A few had already begun loading, vans and trucks backed up to their doors. The loading process would continue well into the night, probably two or three in the morning.

"Alright," he said "let's get this stuff loaded. I'm already behind. Here's your paperwork. Looks like 1,260 pounds."

My estimate for maximum payload had come out to 1,200 pounds, so I would have to rework the numbers. Ken had shown me how to redistribute the weight on paper since they were consistently giving us an extra fifty or one hundred pounds. The client, *Investor's Daily*, was a new newspaper, and as they grew, they had bigger loads to pack into the aircraft. Just as I was flying with flaps that didn't work, I wouldn't turn down an extra hundred pounds. The issue of legality with Cash Air was a non-issue. Just get the job done, no matter what.

The driver started throwing bundles of newspapers through the door. In the crouched position that was all the Navajo allowed, I tried to keep up with him, packing the bundles tightly into the corners of the fuselage.

"Can't you move any faster?" he yelled from outside.

My brow was sweating and my back aching. "Can't help you, pal. I'm doing the best I can," I said defiantly. I wondered why I didn't have the same nerve to respond to Ren.

"Then I may just have to dump them on the ramp for you to load yourself."

"Do what you want, but I won't be able to sign for the load until it's all counted into the airplane," I yelled back.

He swore at me under his breath and kept throwing them in.

"Not much more room in here," I told him, pausing the stacking. "How much more do you have?"

"Six more."

"Okay, they'll go in the nacelles and nose." I stepped out of the airplane and stood up straight to stretch my back. My stomach groaned with hunger—the chocolate bar had long since been eaten.

A voice came from behind the next airplane on the ramp. "I see you're on your own this week, Beth."

It was a familiar voice from the week before, but I couldn't remember his name. "Just had my check ride today as a matter of fact," I responded. The agent put the clipboard in front of me for a signature.

"Air traffic control is assigning slot times to get out of here tonight," the nameless pilot informed me. "Did you file a flight plan?"

"No, it's still VFR."

"There's a line of t-storms out there, you know."

What he said was true, but I was already running late, and if I filed a flight plan, ATC would assign me a departure slot. There would probably be an hour or two wait before I could depart, further delaying my arrival in Buffalo with the freight. Once again, just get the job done. "It's not here yet," I said, "and I can just file in the air."

"You're braver than me," he smiled and turned back to his airplane. He was flying a twin-engine Cessna 310, smaller and a little faster than the Navajo.

It was past midnight, and I was anxious to leave. Maybe the hotel bar would still be open for something to eat if I made good time. I climbed back into the airplane for the last time of the night.

Ten minutes later, the Navajo lifted off the ground after a long takeoff run, this time at maximum gross weight of seven thousand pounds, and then some. The airplane handled differently at this weight, so I tried to feel it out during the climb.

Within minutes of takeoff, I was in turbulent air. Because I was not on a flight plan, the controllers did not provide separation from other aircraft. Thirty miles into the flight, I encountered clouds. Proximity to and flying through clouds was illegal in VFR flight. And nerve-wracking. Maybe that's how the bush pilots of Alaska did it, but this was metro New York, with hundreds of airplanes in its airspace at any given time.

"New York departure, Navajo Niner-Two-Two-Alpha-Charlie." I attempted to contact them between the string of communications with other aircraft already on IFR flight plans.

"Navajo Two-Alpha-Charlie, go ahead."

"Just departed Teterboro VFR. I'd like to file IFR in the air."

"Too busy for that, Two-Alpha-Charlie. You need to file with Millville Flight Service on 122.2."

I dialed in the frequency. "Millville Radio, Navajo Niner-Two-Two-Alpha-Charlie."

No response.

I tried again. "Millville Radio, Navajo Niner-Two-Two-Alpha-Charlie wanting to file IFR."

Still no response. I looked at the weather radar. The line crossed the screen, back and forth like a windshield wiper, set up with a radius of fifty miles. Green, yellow, and red showed the severity of the weather. It showed I was in an area of green with yellow ahead. The way the airplane shook, though, it might as well have been red. I changed my course to find clear air.

"Millville Radio, Navajo Niner-Two-Two-Alpha-Charlie. Please acknowledge," I tried again, checking my chart for another frequency. There still was no response.

In the next moment, Alpha-Charlie flew through the edge of the weather and into the clear.

"Niner-Two-Two-Alpha-Charlie, Millville Radio, do you read?" A voice found its way through the static.

"Roger, Millville."

"Are you ready to file?"

"Negative, Two-Alpha-Charlie will continue VFR." I gambled that the clear air would last all the way to Buffalo. If I flew VFR without a flight plan, I could fly there in a straight line and shave off more time. This was my own bad decision.

"Roger."

The turn back on course was gradual, and I had made no progress to Buffalo with the diversions. The radar, however, showed a clear path ahead with only spots of green weather way off at the edge.

From my present position, the Loran showed a distance of 280 miles to Buffalo with a heading of 310 degrees. At 4,500 feet, my speed over the ground was 150 knots, reminding me that on a westerly course, winds at altitude generally came out of the west. In other words, a headwind. At about the halfway point, I looked off my right wing for the airport beacon at Binghamton. Upstate New York was a dark place at this hour of the night with only widely scattered patches of light on the ground. Binghamton Airport was larger than average, and the beacon was easy to spot. I considered this was my only possibility for getting fuel so late at night without going far out of the way and delaying the newspapers. Still, it was unlikely the fuel operation would be open. If I passed on Binghamton, there had to be enough fuel to make Buffalo.

I passed Binghamton, but not without discomfort. The miles passed slowly, my ground speed never exceeding 155 knots, altitude now two thousand feet as I looked for the least wind. My eyes passed back and forth from the Loran with speed and distance information to the fuel gauges on the panel overhead. There was slightly less than a quarter tank in each of the inboard tanks, and the outboards could be counted as empty. I did the numbers in my head, converting to gallons, then gallons per hour, then time and distance. The calculations gave me no comfort.

Ken had shown me how to lean the fuel mixture for best economy at night by looking at the color of the exhaust manifold on each engine, visible from the cockpit. Gradually pulling back the fuel mixture controls while watching the manifolds, Ken had explained it was not at peak until the metal pipes glowed to a cherry red color. Tonight there was no mistaking how lean my mixture was by those red hot pipes. I thought it might be the one thing that could make the difference.

At fifty miles out, I was tense. I had never seen the fuel gauges in any airplane go down this far, and because they were no more detailed than the fuel gauge in my car, there was no telling how much was left.

At forty miles out, the gauges showed close to empty, with the left one a little less than the right. I cursed myself for saving a few dollars at Teterboro for Ren. It seemed at this point it would be a miracle if I made it to Buffalo.

Steve had told me about a similar scene he played out not too long before. It was in a different aircraft but would still apply here. "When I heard the engine sputter," he told me, "I had my hand on the fuel tank selector ready to switch to the other tank.

The other tank was empty, too, but not as empty as the really empty one. I kept my other hand ready at the fuel pump switch for the extra boost that could give."

I prepared for that.

At thirty miles out, I tuned in Buffalo ATIS. Runway 23 was active with winds out of the west. I would request a straight-in approach to the perpendicular Runway 32. The radios were ready with the tower and ground frequencies tuned in.

At twenty-five miles out, the left engine sputtered. My right hand flew to the fuel selector on the floor, my left hand to the left fuel pump. Switched to the also empty outboard tank, the engine came back to life, albeit a short life. I turned off the fuel pump and replaced my left hand on the yoke, right hand glued to the fuel tank selector. Twenty-three miles to go.

Five more miles passed before the other engine sputtered. My hands moved quickly to do the same as I had for the left engine. It came back. I fixed my eyes on the fuel pressure gauges, the first sign of trouble.

Two miles later, the left one began to die. "Son of a bitch!" I screamed. "Fifteen more miles. Please God, get me there." I switched it back to the original tank, not knowing if that would revive it. But it did.

The next five minutes seemed to take pleasure in their torture. Back and forth on the tanks and engines, my hands flying over the switches, taking thirty seconds of fumes off each tank at a time until it sputtered again. At six miles out, I composed my voice for the call to the tower.

"Buffalo Tower, Navajo Niner-Two-Two-Alpha-Charlie, six miles out for landing with information Echo."

"Roger, Two-Alpha-Charlie, report two-mile left base for Runway 23."

"Tower, Two-Alpha-Charlie requesting straight in for Runway 32. I'm having some problems with my fuel pumps and would like to make it a short approach."

"Roger, that's approved," the male voice said. Then he added, "Is emergency equipment needed at the runway?"

"Negative." *If I even make it to the runway*, I said to myself, *but you're welcome to put the equipment in a field a couple miles short of the runway. If I need it, that's where it's gonna be.*

The runway was in sight now but still four miles to go. The power reduction for landing slowed the sputtering of the engines until finally I could bring my hand up from the floor. Both engines were now running on the outboard tanks, and the fuel pumps were on, for landing or otherwise. I could have cried when my wheels touched the runway but saved it for the hotel room. The last obstacle was to taxi back to the ramp without the engines dying. The only loss there would be of face, and after the night I'd had, that would be nothing.

I made it to the ramp and shut the engines down with panicked relief. On this maiden flight, I had risked so much to prove myself. Prove myself to whom? Prove myself to what end? Prove myself at what cost? The questions were there, and I learned a few lessons. But I still had my eyes on the ultimate goal.

The fuel truck pulled in front as I opened the pilot door. It felt as though weeks had passed since the door had been my problem.

"Inboards and outboards?" the fueler asked me through the door.

"Fill 'em all," I said, "and tell me how much you put in each side." The van pulled up to the plane, and the ground agent began helping himself to my cargo. "There's more in the nose and nacelles, too," I shouted to the back of the plane.

I leaned back on the headrest and closed my eyes. Only when the fueler knocked on the side of the plane did I open them again.

"I've never put this much fuel into a Chieftain," he announced with a degree of awe. "Over 189 gallons."

I just nodded. The total usable fuel for the Chieftain was 182 gallons. Total capacity was 192 gallons. That meant it had gone well into the unusable fuel, and there were less than three gallons left of that. I probably couldn't have gone another mile.

Surely, in all my poor judgment, I was blessed with someone's watchful eye.

CHAPTER 16

Please, No More

"How was your first night?" Fred was as cheerful as when he left me off eight hours earlier.

"Oh, God," I groaned, "don't ask."

"What's the matter? Did something happen?"

"A lot of things happened, but right now I'd rather just forget about it."

"Hey, that's okay. I understand." He was trying to be kind.

"Is the bar still open at the hotel?" I asked.

"It really was a bad night, huh?"

"A drink would help, but I'm really looking for something to eat. I haven't had anything all night."

"Yeah, they're open till three. They've got the best buffalo wings around." He pulled up to the entrance. "I'm done at two, ya know. How about I buy you a beer?"

"No thanks, Fred. I can't tell if I'm more tired or hungry and I think the tired part is going to win."

"Maybe some other night this week when you've had a better night?"

"Sure." I forced a smile. He had no idea what a sobering night it had been.

Dragging my flight bag and my body down the long hall to my room, I thought Alpha-Charlie must have felt the same way during those last miles to Buffalo. I turned the key in the door and opened it, throwing my things on the floor. I leaned against the wall and slid to the floor. For five minutes, ten minutes, I held myself tightly, legs gathered to my chest, and sobbed. My body shook as I lay on the floor. The sobs were endless, coming from deep inside and uncontrollable.

When I finally stopped crying, I slowly released the tight hold I had on myself and lay quietly on the grimy carpet for a while, thankful for the quiet and absence of terror. I was exhausted in every way and could have slept right there on the floor had the red light not been flashing on the phone. I stumbled to the bed and fell back on it where I had slept that afternoon. The lady at the front desk had a message—Steve had called. Call him in Chicago between 2 and 3 a.m. It was 2:25.

The phone number was in my wallet, neatly folded in a secure section in front of my pilot licenses. The number at the Chicago hotel rang and rang. A groggy voice finally answered after the sixth ring.

"Midway Gardens."

"Room 332, please," I said, trying not to sound like I had been crying.

She transferred me.

"Hello," an unfamiliar voice answered after two rings.

"Is Steve there?" I asked.

"Yup, hold on."

"Hello." This time it was Steve's voice.

"Hi Steve, it's me. What's going on?" I was happy to hear his voice. Its familiarity was comforting.

"Okay." He sounded glad I had called. "What time did you get back?"

"Just a little while ago. How's Chicago?" I did not want him to ask me how my night went.

"I didn't fly tonight. Harry's out here, and he wanted to do one of the runs himself, so I got a night off."

"Then what are you doing up so late?"

"Well, I didn't want to change my body clock," he explained. "You know what I mean now that you're doing the Buffalo run. Sleep all day and fly all night."

"Which route are you doing?"

"Chicago to Cleveland to Columbus and back. It's the shorter of the two routes. But the reason I called is to ask you about your check ride. How'd it go?"

I let out a little laugh. "Well, I passed, so I guess it went well."

"Yeah, but what did you have to do for maneuvers? What I'm asking is, was it as much of a joke as mine was?"

"You didn't tell me about yours, but mine couldn't have been any easier than it was. I just flew from Lawrence to Buffalo with Harry, and that was it. Why are you asking?"

"I just have a bad feeling about this whole thing," he said with unusual concern. "You know, Ren and Harry, and the airplanes and routes we're flying. It's growing too fast."

"What do you mean?" I asked, too depleted from the night's events to give it deep thought.

"I see nothing good coming out of it all. Everything we do every night is illegal in some way. Every time I'm out on a ramp, I'm wondering if the Feds will show up and go through the airplane. Let me tell you, they'd find plenty to write up. That would be the end of my license, just like Adam's."

Since when did Steve worry about things like this, and why did he have to lay this on me at two-thirty in the morning? "Are you going to quit?"

"Of course not," he replied. "I'm just going to rack up as many multi-engine hours as I can while the company is still going and then get out and get a real job with the airlines."

I was beginning to wonder if we all would make it that far without losing our licenses…or worse.

There were voices in the background, and Steve answered them.

"I'd better go," he said. "They're back now, and I want to see how things went. Love you."

He hung up before I could say goodbye, and I sat on the bed feeling worse than before. Before the call, I could have slept through the night, morning, and even into the early afternoon. Now it seemed that sleep might not come at all.

CHAPTER 17

Teterboro Nights

By Thursday, I found it hard to imagine flying *with* flaps. In fact, it was hard to imagine flying with a lot of things, such as the autopilot, the ADF, some of the cockpit lights, and more. All of these things should have been marked as "inoperable" in the aircraft logs, and if so, each was cause for grounding the airplane until fixed. But Ren had made it clear the first night of the week that the only way a small Part 135 charter company could survive was to be blind to certain regulations, and because small charter companies were the only way for us to get the multi-engine flying time we needed to get the "real job," there were few qualms about taking off each night without operable flaps so that five more hours could be logged after landing. Steve was doing the same in Chicago and keeping the complaints to himself. We were getting the multi-engine time we wanted and needed.

Steve and I were not the only ones on this crazy ride. All of Ren's pilots saddled up airplanes plagued with broken equipment each night. Drew Petrucci was the only one who left Cash Air, probably for this reason. He took a similar job with another charter company in Buffalo and heard it was as bad as Cash Air. I had also heard other freight pilots in Buffalo and

Teterboro talking about the Part 135 companies they worked for, and the corners they also cut in aircraft maintenance, so I accepted it as the norm.

I did the shallow approach into Teterboro required for the no-flap landing and touched down just before dark. Four nights without dinner had been enough, so I had left Buffalo early this time to land in Teterboro before the restaurants out on the main road closed. There were plenty out there if you didn't mind the walk.

Peter Covich's Seneca was parked on the ramp, and he was checking the oil in the right engine. I taxied to the spot next to him.

"You're early tonight!" he greeted me as I stepped out onto the wing. We had spent our waiting hours together most of this week, his happy, handsome face making good company during the long night hours. Peter had wavy, thick blond hair, short and neat. In fact, everything about Peter was always neat, from his unwrinkled shirts and jeans, to his clean, white sneakers.

"On purpose," I said. "I couldn't stand another night with just a candy bar. Want to take a walk and get some dinner?"

"Sure beats fighting for a seat in the lounge."

The restaurant was small and dark, more a bar than a restaurant. A large, greasy burger with Swiss cheese and mushrooms was placed in front of me. The same for Peter without the mushrooms.

"How's Steve getting along in Chicago?" he asked.

I bit into the burger, and some mushrooms dropped to the plate. "Doing okay, I guess. I haven't seen him in a couple weeks." It surprised me how anxious I was to dissociate myself from Steve when a good-looking guy was sitting across the table. Peter was everything Steve was not, and even though I missed

Steve and believed I loved him, it was refreshing to spend time with Peter.

He smiled. Perhaps he understood.

"I guess the Chicago routes are going okay," I continued. More mushrooms slid out, and I pushed them back with my fork. "There haven't been any problems, just that the loads are always heavy, so Ren wants me out there next week. I'm the lightest pilot he's got by about fifty pounds," I explained, "so he figures I can add that much more weight to the Chicago load."

"Since when does Ren care about fifty pounds, or even more? Every one of his flights goes out overweight."

I shrugged. "Yeah, I know. He's a strange little man who runs a strange little company." I took another bite of my burger. "I thought I heard him say you'd be out there, too."

His mouth was full, but he nodded enthusiastically while swallowing. "They're adding another route, so I might get to stay there for a few weeks anyway. It's such a great opportunity. I'm getting multi-engine time a lot sooner and a lot faster than I ever would have otherwise. If it wasn't for Ren, I'd still be an instructor. But now I'm flying a Seneca, and at this rate, I'll be in a Navajo pretty soon."

I smiled. Peter made it all seem so good. I didn't want to spoil it by mentioning Steve's concerns and gripes.

CHAPTER 18

When the Sky Turns Green

Thunderstorms are green. There is no mistaking it, even at
night. When the color of the sky around you takes on that
green cast, calm air soon ends with a loud bang.

With the arrival of summer, thunderstorms grew all over
the flat Midwestern states. They grew tall and mean, sometimes
topping out at 40,000 or 50,000 feet above the ground, or even
more. By day, we could look up to see how far they reached
before they engulfed us in them, but at night, standing on the
ramp preparing for flight, we could only guess. It didn't matter, though, because our only hope for avoiding them was to
fly around or maybe underneath them. When it was time for
takeoff, we had to rely on the telephone weather briefing, information from the controllers on the ground, and what we could
glean from the primitive three-color weather radar in each of
Ren's planes. The challenge was to stay away from the storms,
but often we couldn't, and each of us knew exactly how fright-
ening it was to penetrate one of these massive beasts.

For almost three weeks in Chicago now, I had been working
hard just as the other pilots to avoid the green clouds by flying
VFR without a flight plan. Even though the air traffic controllers worked with the pilots to avoid being steered right into the

heart of those storms, the controlled nature of an IFR flight plan increased the likelihood. At 1,500 or 2,000 feet, I could often be sure of staying below them, and when that didn't work out, I still had the three-color weather radar to help maneuver out of them.

Of the two routes being flown out of Chicago's Midway Airport, I flew the longer one. Each night at about ten o'clock, I departed with a full load of *Investor's Daily* newspapers and traveled the 850 miles to Kansas City and then to St. Louis before returning to Chicago between two and three in the morning. Steve flew the other route to Cleveland and Columbus, and Ken relieved each of us two nights a week.

It was just the three of us in Chicago this week, four if we counted Lou Janicki. He was our ground coordinator, an employee of *Investor's Daily*, the man we could always count on to make sure the freight was on time and help load it.

At two thirty on an early Friday morning in late June, I buttoned up the airplane while Ken secured the wheels with chocks. He had flown Steve's route and waited with Lou for me to land so we could return to the hotel together. Even though he lived in Chicago, Lou stayed with us in the hotel most nights because of the late hours. Between the four of us, we shared two rooms. Sometimes there were five of us, and we still shared two rooms. Ren was cheap.

"What's the matter, Lou, didn't you get enough sleep while you were waiting for us?" Ken needled him.

Lou yawned loudly. He was easy to like if you didn't sleep in the same room with him. When that happened, he slept, and you didn't. The rhythm of his snores, farts, and mumbling went on through the night.

"Alright, let's go," I said and picked up my flight bag.

"White Castle?" Lou asked as he did every night before we went back to the hotel. "I'm starving." He laid a hand on his thick waist.

"As usual," Ken responded.

We walked through the general aviation terminal to get to the parking lot. The woman at the desk glared at us. As freight pilots, the lowest caste in the flying world, we were not allowed in this new building that comprised Phoenix Aviation. There was a small, dark room in the old building attached to the hangar for us, but we ignored that rule each night before and after our flights. The staff had become powerless in eliminating our presence, though some nights they asked us to leave the building. Did we soil the new furniture? Or perhaps we dropped peanuts from the candy machine on the carpet. Maybe we embarrassed them with our freight pilot attire, suited to checking oil and testing fuel in our ratty airplanes. Or it could have been as simple as the fact that we weren't jet pilots. Whatever the reason, night after night we sat on the sofas, and night after night, they glared at us with increasing irritation.

"Anything exciting happen tonight, Lou?" I asked from the front seat of the rental car. Lou sat in the back while Ken drove.

He yawned again. "Nope, not a thing."

"I talked to Harry earlier tonight," Ken said, "and he told me that Peter won't be coming back out here. He still needs him back east to do the Teterboro route with the Seneca."

The news was a disappointment. Peter had spent the previous week with us in Chicago. He came out as a backup for the heavy loads we were getting, but Ren called the day before while we were at the airport and instructed Peter to fly back to Lawrence right away. Ren needed him for the new Boston route. There wasn't even time for him to go back to the hotel to get his duffle bag.

"We need him here, Ren," Ken had insisted. "What do you want us to do with the extra load? Turn it down?"

"Just tell him to get in the airplane and get back here." Ren would not budge.

"Whatever you say."

"And Ken," Ren added before hanging up, "don't leave any newspapers behind. I'm counting on you to make sure these routes don't get screwed up."

Ken turned the corner into White Castle, the closest, fastest, latest, cheapest food available. Inside, the walls and lights were shocking white, and my eyes had difficulty adjusting.

"Order enough for Steve, too," I said, squinting. "He'll probably be awake."

"Twelve cheeseburgers, four fries, four orange sodas," Ken ordered.

Lou took the bags of food, and we walked back to the car. "So what are you gonna do when the loads go over?" Lou asked.

"The same thing we do every night," I answered. "Stuff it in somewhere and get it where it needs to go. It would just be nice to know that if an engine quits on takeoff, I'd be able to keep the plane in the air long enough to get back to the runway. With the extra weight you're giving us, we all know that's not going to happen."

Lou was not a pilot, so he wasn't sure how to respond.

"Don't forget that first night, Beth," Ken said, "when you and I flew the route together." He was talking about my orientation on the Kansas City–St. Louis route with him. The newspapers arrived late, so we left the paperwork for later. When we rolled for takeoff, three quarters of a six-thousand-foot runway was behind us before I could even coax it into the air. It was a heavy load, a very heavy load. "Do you remember what I said after that flight, Beth?" Ken continued, turning into the hotel parking lot.

"How could I forget?"

"What?" Lou asked impatiently, frustrated because he didn't remember.

"Come on, Lou," Ken pushed him. "How could you forget about that?"

Lou looked at him blankly. He really did not remember. But, as always, he was not a pilot and couldn't fully grasp the consequences.

"For God's sake, Lou, we left the ramp 900 pounds overweight that night! An airplane with a max gross weight of 6,500 pounds took off at 7,400 pounds! That could have been deadly."

He parked the car, and we went in through the back entrance. It was always quiet this time of night. Even the train tracks so busy during the day with hundreds of freight cars were quiet.

"So are you gonna start turnin' the extra freight away?" Lou was concerned.

Ken pushed the button for the elevator. "I don't mind taking an extra one or two hundred pounds," he said, "but not nine hundred pounds. And I am only speaking for myself. If Beth turns it down, that's her decision as pilot in command."

There was silence in the elevator as our three tired faces stared at the numbers above the door. It was only two floors up, but the old elevator moved slowly. Knowing my bed was just down the hall, I allowed my eyelids to become heavy. No longer did the cockpit require my undivided attention.

It was also the only time of the day when the laughter died down, to return the next day until we loaded our airplanes and left. The sleep we got was just enough to not be enough. Ken joked that we were actually part of a sleep deprivation study that Ren and Harry were secretly conducting. Because we were beyond tired, we laughed about almost anything. Even Steve laughed a little.

The final walk down the hall for the night always seemed to take longer than during the day. The numbers on the doors increased slowly, and only the food in the bags Lou carried kept our pace from slowing to a crawl. It was the third meal of the day for us, or rather, it was the first. The second and third were in the hotel restaurant or at the Greek diner down the street. On Saturday nights, the one night when none of us flew, we drank beer with dinner leaving us even giddier, at least until the next morning.

Ken turned the key in the lock of the first door. The second one opened when Steve heard us, and he stepped out.

"We've got food," I told him.

"I need to talk to you." He had a serious look on his face.

"To me?" I pointed to myself.

"Everyone."

Ken and I glanced at each other questioningly, and the three of us followed Steve into the room. He sat on the bed by the nightstand. Notes were scribbled and scattered by the phone. I sat at the foot of the bed, Lou in the chair by the window, and Ken stood.

"What's up?" Ken asked. He wanted to eat.

Steve looked at me and said, "You know how I've said to you that something would go wrong with this company?"

"Uh huh…"

"Well, it happened tonight. Ren called a little while ago. Peter crashed in Boston tonight."

I gasped and a chill shot through me. A horrified hush filled the room.

"He's dead."

Ken gasped. "Oh, my God."

Lou's face dropped, and my voice cracked with disbelief.

"What happened?" I asked with desperation.

"It's too early to know. It just happened about an hour ago."

Just an hour ago. The closeness of the time made it all too real, too close. I had just landed about an hour ago. My thoughts scattered. My mind could not absorb what Steve had just told us.

"He was on his way into Boston from Teterboro," Steve filled in some of the blanks. "On the approach. It's IFR in Boston tonight, about six hundred feet overcast, but the visibility is good—about eight miles," he said. I looked at him questioningly and he explained. "I called Flight Service for the weather there after Ren called me."

"Where on the approach did it happen?" Ken asked. He was desperate to understand what could have gone wrong when Peter was so close to landing.

"Don't know. I watched the story on television when it broke on the news. They said he crashed into a neighborhood in Dorchester, and the fire is still burning now, a nine-alarm fire."

This was too much to hear. We were sitting in a hotel room in Chicago while Peter lay dead in an inferno that was still burning. Just the day before, I said goodbye to Peter before he flew the Seneca back to Boston. Peter was so high on flying and airplanes and the hours he was accumulating. I sat on the wing of his Seneca before he got in to start the engines, wished him a good flight back, and told him to get back to Chicago as soon as he could. "See ya, kid," he smiled at me. "Remember to have fun."

For a long time, the room was dead quiet with only occasional groans and murmurs. No one moved, each of us trying somehow to make sense of it.

"Anybody want to eat this stuff?" Ken finally asked. He held it over the trash can. "I don't want it."

Lou and I shook our heads. Steve didn't answer.

———

The night was long, and none of us really slept. The phone didn't ring with more news. There were long periods of silence interspersed with brief questions for which there were no answers. I shifted between the bed, the window, and the hall. Feelings ranged from utter shock to deep hurt and sadness for Peter to realization of the danger in what we were doing each night, or at least in the way we did it. We all felt invincible with an arrogance that only comes with youth and immaturity. Just as Peter was the victim tonight, I could have been the victim so many other times. We all knew Peter did not have enough hours logged to fly legally under instrument flight conditions for a Part 135 company. For that, he needed 1,200 hours. And for that, he now had paid the price of his life.

I finally fell asleep on top of the bedspread as the sun was coming up. Ken was asleep on the other bed, and Steve and Lou were in the other room. We awoke two hours later when the phone rang. I reached for it from the bed, my body aching.

"Hello," I answered, barely audible.

"It's Ren." His voice was weary. "I don't have any more information. There isn't a fucking clue as to what happened. The reason I'm calling is to tell you that the Feds will be crawling all over this place today, examining us with a goddamned microscope. Keep flying, no matter what, unless I tell you to stop. They'll probably be out there in Chicago, too, to take a close look at all of you and the airplanes. You got nothing to hide, and if they give you a hard time, just tell them to fuck off." Ren was running scared. Peter was dead and maybe even others on the ground.

"Okay. We'll keep flying, but let us know as soon as you find anything out," I said.

There was nothing more to say, and we hung up. Ken and I sat facing each other on opposite beds, and I repeated what Ren said. Our eyes met somewhere in the middle, and I lost my control. The tears began to flow. Ken moved to my side and held me as we both cried.

CHAPTER 19

The Wreckage

We quietly gathered in one of the hotel rooms with the newspaper articles sent from home by Ken's wife. Bits and pieces of information came to us during the days following the crash. There was some coverage in the Chicago papers, but most information came over the phone from the people back home. When the packet of news articles arrived at the front desk, we pored over them with horror. Coverage of the accident in Boston was intense, day after day making front page news as facts and questions surfaced.

We learned that Peter's plane clipped one triple-decker house and then crashed into another just after one in the morning, just three miles short of the runway at Boston Logan Airport. He had radioed in at the marker beacon over Milton, Massachusetts on the approach. Fifteen seconds later, he disappeared from Air Traffic Control radar.

A nine-alarm fire engulfed triple-decker homes and at least seven automobiles, and it took 150 firefighters and thirty trucks a full hour to control it. Three houses in the congested Dorchester neighborhood burned to the ground, the one Peter crashed into along with the two on either side. Cars exploded in the fire, and the intense heat damaged other houses. Miraculously, there were no other deaths, only injuries.

And when the fire had stopped, only rubble remained. Pieces of aircraft were strewn from one side of the street to the other along with half-burned bundles of the *Investor's Daily* newspapers and cancelled checks he was carrying…and Peter's unrecognizable body wedged between the burned-out shells of two cars. One of the Seneca engine propellers was seen jutting out from a burned-out car with melted tires. We would later learn that the crash may have been caused when the Seneca's nose compartment door became unhinged and sliced through the airplane windshield, decapitating Peter.

The crash made national news, from Boston to New York to Washington to Los Angeles and beyond.

How poignantly fatal the sky can be. Not giving it due respect, though, we continued to tempt fate, never knowing the terror felt by the unlucky ones before their deaths. If we did know, if what Peter saw and felt on that unholy night was not a secret, perhaps prudence and caution would have played a more prominent role in what we did. But only the end result, ruined lives amidst the wreckage, was left as a warning.

"It says here the Feds are questioning whether Peter met the time requirements for the flight," Ken told us from his seat by the window. In the corner behind him lay the duffle bag that Peter never brought back to Boston with him. A clean shirt and a bottle of shampoo sat on top. None of us had touched it since that night, leaving it as a sort of shrine to him. "They're saying that his age was enough for them to know he could not have had the hours required."

"They still have to document it," Steve pointed out.

"And they will," Ken said, "as soon as they get hold of his logbooks and talk to the people he used to fly with."

I came to a paragraph on the page in my lap that made me swallow hard. "The FAA will be reviewing all the pilots, all thirteen of us. It says so right here." We were each guilty of some violation while flying for Cash Air.

"It's just a matter of time before they shut us down," Ken stated. "Half the pilots back home have already quit."

Ken was right, and we all knew it, but we were isolated in Chicago, and our routes were the mainstay of Ren's operation, so we continued. Ren or Harry called each day with news and hopeless words of inspiration—generally righteous words defying the findings of the NTSB, denying any wrongdoing. The fact was that Ron was running scared. If he could salvage this mess, it would cost a lot of money, and even then, he would probably lose the contract with *Investor's Daily*.

My own violations were the same as everyone else's. Not enough hours, flying airplanes with broken equipment, taking off overweight. The list was long, and there was nothing I could do to change or correct it. I knew I had to clean up my own act, but we were all still mired in the nightmare that was called Cash Air. My innermost fear—and that of every one of us—was that this would be the end of my dream to make it to the airlines.

The investigation would go on for many months, and for Ren, it was highly controversial. Based on the autopsy report, Ren maintained Peter's decapitation caused the airplane's demise, but the NTSB ultimately attributed the cause of the accident to pilot error, insufficient pilot experience, and operator (Cash Air) failure to comply with procedures and directives.

———

The phone call came one week later, two weeks after the crash. The FAA had completed their initial investigation. They suspended Cash Air's operating license based on the findings. They found the meters on two of the airplanes had been tampered with to extend required maintenance checks. Records of pilot ground and flight training had been falsified. Two flights had carried hazardous materials even though the pilots had not received hazmat training. And five of the thirteen pilots on Cash Air's payroll were found not to have the flight time required for Part 135 instrument flight. The FAA found no issues in my own records, and I went unnoticed.

The FAA shut the company down. Ren told us to pack our things and bring the airplanes home. We returned from Chicago unemployed.

CHAPTER 20

Back to Beverly

Sobered and unsure, we went back to Massachusetts after the FAA shut down Cash Air. It was the summer of 1987, and back at New England Flyers, Rod rehired us as flight instructors. He hadn't added any new instructors since we left to tow banners for Brian, and because we were returning in the summer, we had the benefit of a busy flight school. We took any and all flying Rod could give us.

The atmosphere at the flight school was the same as before, except that there was a solemnness in the room whenever the subject of Cash Air was mentioned.

The airport bums still gathered each day to share their war stories and airport gossip and drink Rod's booze. Students came and went, and Adam was working the line. He had lost his license after the stolen plane and flying under the influence incident, but he also learned his lesson. He stopped drinking and started over earning his licenses and ratings.

And, of course, there was the Cub. Steve and I still had our shares, and we made sure to fly her whenever we could, before students, between students, and after students.

So, it was on a sunny Sunday afternoon in early August that I collected my flight gear after finishing with my last student of the day and crossed the ramp to the same tie-down spot the Cub had occupied since her arrival. She had just returned from her annual maintenance at the service hangar on the field, the first annual since Rod brought the Cub down from New Hampshire.

In the usual way, I positioned myself in front to hand-prop her for our flight. One pull, two pulls, and then the engine started smoothly. I walked back to untie the tail, then the left wing, and then the right wing.

As I untied the right wing, the airplane engine surged and jumped over the chocks that were the final restraint. The Cub lunged forward with determination instead of idling in place as expected. My brain sprung into fight-or-flight mode, and I chose to fight, adrenaline screaming through my body. I grabbed the right wing strut to try to hold the airplane back, but it had more force than I did and dragged me away from the tie-down spot onto the pavement of the taxiway.

I kept fighting, holding onto the strut in a struggle to stop the movement. It wasn't working. My back was scraped bare as the Cub dragged me mercilessly. I knew I was losing the fight. Then, about a hundred feet up the taxiway, I couldn't hold on any longer and let go, dumped on the taxiway. I watched with panic as the Cub continued her march across another taxiway, finally tumbling to a halt in the ravine beyond.

I didn't even feel the pain in my back as I stood up from the tarmac. Finally upright, I stared ahead, gaping at the wrecked Cub, her engine now silenced.

I ran back across the ramp to the office. Rod, Steve, and Adam were standing outside surveying the scene. The controllers in the tower would have seen it all. Rod and Steve would at least have seen the final crash, and everyone else with a view of the airport that day would have seen it, too.

"It jumped the chocks," I rushed to explain what happened.

"Jesus," Rod said, shaking his head.

Steve just stood there looking very unhappy. I wished he would say something, anything.

"I did everything as we usually do," I pleaded. "Why would this happen?"

Rod sighed. "They probably tweaked the throttle during the maintenance, made it idle higher."

So it wasn't really my fault? I looked over at Steve, still staring at the Cub in the distance.

"I'll call the mechanics to get equipment to haul it over to the maintenance hangar," Rod announced and went inside.

Steve finally turned his head and looked at me. "What a fuckup," he said with contempt.

My body was still shaking, but it was clear Steve had no compassion. I turned and followed Rod into the office. The back of my shirt was ripped, and my back stung. Adam came in behind me.

"I have a spare T-shirt you can put on," Adam offered. "Do you need help cleaning your back?"

Our roles were reversed since the day I had bailed Adam out of jail. Now it was my turn to cry and be scared, and Adam assumed his new role with kindness.

I nodded, and we went into the bathroom together with a towel and a clean shirt. He gently dabbed the scrapes on my back with the towel, now damp with cold water, careful not to make it hurt.

"It's not your fault, Beth," he said. "You did everything in the usual way. It's just that you were the first to prop it since the maintenance—it would have happened to Steve if he was out there."

Adam was right, but it didn't change the fact that the Cub would be out of commission for a while. And that meant the other owners would not be happy, especially Steve.

———

By four thirty, they had removed the Cub from the ditch to the maintenance hangar. The atmosphere in the flight school was more somber than ever, but the usual crowd still gathered for their version of happy hour. Steve took part but still looked unhappy, at least with me.

I needed to get out of there and be alone. "I'm heading home," I announced to anyone listening as I grabbed my bag.

Steve didn't answer.

I was halfway to my car when I realized he was following me out.

"Hey," he yelled for my attention.

I stopped and looked back at him.

"Don't think you can just walk away from this," he shouted as he approached me. "You fucked up. You wrecked the Cub. My airplane."

"What are you talking about? It's my airplane, too, along with nine other people," I responded, anger rising inside me. "And what happened today would have happened to anyone who took it out today." After this day from hell, my patience was thin. "You heard what Rod said about the throttle."

I turned to continue walking to the car, but Steve grabbed my arm and stopped me.

"Don't grab me!" I pulled my arm away. There was an anger is his manner I hadn't ever seen before. "What's wrong with you?"

He raised his hand and struck the left side of my face with force. The impact of his hand was loud, and my bag fell to the ground as I reeled back. I barely caught my balance and held my hand to my cheek.

"You're an idiot," he said and turned back to the flight school.

Shock and confusion soon made way for silent tears as I watched him walk away. It wasn't his usual loping walk; instead, it was a posture of anger and aggression.

CHAPTER 21

Dead Flies

No one had ever hit me before, and the emotions that followed conflicted between anger, shame, and sadness. Steve apologized for hitting me the next day, and even though it was a weak apology, he seemed sincere. Everything soon went back to the usual routine, and the incident was no longer discussed, as if it was taboo, especially after the Cub was repaired and back to flying. As it had been since the start of this career, my life involved only two things—Steve and flying—and somehow, way back in the beginning of my flight lessons, the two had become inextricably intertwined.

I knew I had to separate myself from him, so I gradually moved my job search further and further away from Massachusetts, with letters and resumes in the mail as far as California. I didn't know if I could follow through with my hypothetical plan—and it would have been difficult to pack and leave alone—but I kept reminding myself what was best was not always easy.

A response finally came from Burlington, Vermont. Frank Dunning, Chief Pilot for Mountain Air Services—a freight and passenger air charter company—asked me to come up for an interview and a test flight. This was a big step, and the next day I drove the four hours to Vermont. I didn't tell Steve.

———

"Nice job. You handled the airplane well," Frank told me after the flight test.

We stood on the ramp outside Mountain Air's building that housed the offices along with the cleanest hangar space I had ever seen. I didn't know a Part 135 operation could be so professional.

"Thank you." My hopes were high.

"Your movements of the controls are smooth, and that's important when there are people in the airplane. I learned to fly that way in the Air Force. Couldn't get through a flight check if we weren't smooth. I'm retired but I try to pass on all I learned to the young people I hire," he explained. "I know you've been flying freight before this. It's easy to get sloppy when you only have boxes in the back. Our business here at Mountain Air is half and half, passengers and freight, so we expect you always to fly as though you're carrying passengers."

Did he mean I had the job? It sure sounded that way. "How many airplanes do you have?" I asked.

"We've got the four Navajos, a single-engine Cessna, two Beech Barons, and a Piper Aztec." The operation was impressive. "And Joe Fontaine—he's the owner of the company—keeps the Stearman over there for his own fun." He pointed to the yellow biplane in back of the hangar. "When would you be available to start?"

"Immediately. I'm not working now."

"Okay then, I'll call you within the week once we've made our decision."

Driving home the same day, I was excited, even elated. I did it alone, and no one knew about it. Until that night when I collapsed and told Steve. The next day, he called Mountain Air, and the day after that he had an interview with Frank. I had ruined my chances. When Frank called Steve to offer him the job, Steve called me with the news.

"Great news!" he announced. "I got the job at Mountain Air."

"What?!" I uttered, my voice drowned out by the angry screams sounding in my head. "Then I guess I didn't get it."

"You never know. Maybe he's hiring more than one pilot. And if not, you can still go up there with me and look for a job somewhere else on the field. You could always instruct— Mountain Air has a flight school, too, you know." It was a weak attempt to make me feel better. He did not see a need to apologize or even hide his excitement. I ended the conversation quickly. How could I have been so stupid to even tell him about the job? I was disgusted with myself and spent the evening crying and screaming into my pillow. Everything that was mine became his. Except for Cash Air. He shared that with me, and it ended in disaster.

The next afternoon, as I considered my next move, the phone rang. It was Frank. "As you probably know, Beth, we've hired your friend, Steve, for the position. After discussing it, though, we'd like to have you on board up here at Mountain Air, too," he explained. "I spoke with Joe, and we've decided we really could use two more pilots instead of just one, so if you're interested, I'd like to offer it to you."

It was a bittersweet surprise, a bandage to patch up my pride. "Thank you, Frank. I'd be thrilled to take the position."

The thrill was questionable, and I waited two days before telling Steve I would also be flying for Mountain Air.

—

We stood under damp, cloudy skies in front of the North Hero General Store in Vermont. Steve glanced at his new watch, the congratulatory gift he bought for himself a week before.

"Looks like it'll be a forty-minute drive to Burlington," he estimated, "if you don't get stuck behind some farmer on his tractor."

We got back in our cars, each filled with all the belongings that could be folded and stuffed into the tiny interiors, and continued to the house we found just three days earlier. Actually, it had been my find, just as Mountain Air was. There was a tiny ad in a local paper. We had driven up from Massachusetts for just one day, and I hoped to return at the end of it with two leases signed and a new address for each of us. Instead, it ended up as one new address in North Hero for both of us.

"It's too big for one person," Steve had insisted after we walked through the house with the owner.

"What difference does it make?" I argued. "The rent is cheap enough."

"Yeah, but it makes more sense to split the rent and share it. Why waste the money?" He knew how to manipulate me, and so he did. This time, though, it was only because Steve wanted me to pay half the rent. He was cheap. It was not because he wanted to be with me or live with me. "How about this—we'll take it together until you can find a place in Burlington."

I agreed, but not without reserve. *It will be temporary*, I told myself. *I will start looking for another place, my own place, right away.* Since the day the Cub was wrecked, I knew I had to put some distance between Steve and me, but I couldn't bring myself to break up with him and just end it. There was a part of me deep inside still needing and wanting what he didn't have to give.

Living in the same apartment with Steve was difficult to imagine, but living in Vermont was not at all difficult. I looked forward to the new start. Vermont had been my home for four years in college. For me, it was a homecoming.

Steve pulled into the gravel driveway of the white, two-family house, and I pulled in behind him. Horses and cows grazed in the backfield, and the barn door was open. We were in the tiny town of North Hero, Vermont, located on an island in Lake Champlain, just a few miles from the Canadian border.

I stepped out of the car and sized up my new home for only the second time. It was empty inside, not even carpet on the floors. Downstairs, a large living room opened into an equally large kitchen. Upstairs, there were two bedrooms and the only bathroom. I walked from room to room while Steve unloaded his car.

"It's dirtier than I remember," I said from the bathroom as Steve walked by. When we had seen the apartment three days earlier, I had looked at it as if it would be mine alone, and from that perspective, it looked great. After we signed the lease together, the image in my mind changed.

Steve didn't answer. All I could hear were the sounds from the bedroom. When I turned the faucet handle, the water spurted out as if it hadn't been run in a long time. It ran a rusty orange color for a few seconds and then cleared. The smell of sulfur was strong.

"Will the water always smell this bad?" I asked.

"It's well water. What do you expect?"

Steve came out of the bedroom. "Let's finish unloading the cars."

"You unload, I'll start cleaning. It's going to take a while."

"Make sure you get rid of the dead flies."

A few minutes later, Steve came back upstairs carrying a futon. There was an unspoken understanding that we would share it. The other bedroom, the larger of the two, was for boxes. For furniture, there was an antique table from my grandparents' basement. On the table would sit a pale green hurricane lamp from my childhood bedroom. Other than that, the wood floor was bare, and we had nothing to hang on the walls.

The cars were now empty, and the apartment still felt hollow. I pretended not to notice, focusing only on the window sills still covered with dead flies.

CHAPTER 22

Settling In

"Vermont's a cool place," Pat Fitzpatrick said. He sat next to his wife, also Pat, at the card table set up in our living and/or dining room. "The only thing missing up here is Mexican food. We'd move back to Florida just for that."

Pat, his wife, laughed in agreement. He smiled, so I figured he was joking. They moved from Florida several months earlier when Pat finished his time in the Navy as a helicopter pilot. Because his fixed-wing time was low and his goal had always been to fly for the airlines, he took the job at Mountain Air to build the fixed-wing time he needed. Pat and Pat sold their house in Jacksonville, packed their lives into the car, and headed north for this job.

"Then what you're saying is you wouldn't have taken the job if you knew there weren't many Mexican restaurants in Vermont?" Steve asked.

"Definitely not," Pat responded.

We laughed. Six of us sat in the mostly empty room. Lyle Tibbetts occupied the other chair at the small table. He was one of the flight instructors at Mountain Air. He was the youngest and looked the youngest, too, tall and thin, with no need to shave the blond fuzz on his boyish face.

I sat on the floor up against a pile of boxes with Paul DuBois, Mountain Air's lineman and aspiring charter pilot. He was about my age and Steve's height. He already had his private and instrument licenses but was still working on the remaining licenses and ratings and the hours to go with them, the same place I was in when working the line for Rod.

It was the end of the second week in Vermont for Steve and me, and we decided to have a get-together with the people we now saw each day in the office and on the ramp.

"You wouldn't have come all the way up here if there was a company this good down there," I said to Pat. "Mountain Air is unusual in this business."

"That's because there's a lot of money behind it," Steve added. That seemed to turn him on.

"Yeah, and that's because Joe Fontaine owns it," Pat completed the story.

Steve leaned forward in his seat. "Hey, did I tell you I picked up Joe in White Plains the other day for his weekend in Vermont? He handed me a fifty-dollar tip at the end."

Pat raised his eyebrows. "Not surprising," he said, "I heard him telling Frank you were the smoothest pilot he's ever flown with."

I listened without a word, thinking only of what Frank had told me when my training was complete.

"You did well, Beth," Frank told me in his office after signing the paperwork that made me legal to fly for Mountain Air. "But I want you to fly only the scheduled freight runs for the first couple of weeks, just until you're more comfortable with the equipment. Don't get me wrong now. There are no problems at all, but you don't have as much experience as Steve and the other pilots."

I had tried to swallow it with dignity. "Which are the scheduled runs?" I asked.

"They're two nice, easy runs," Frank explained gently. "One goes in a Navajo early in the morning to Albany, and the other goes in the Aztec to Montreal in the evening."

For the next week, I had flown to Albany and back in the early morning, leaving the rest of the day free until I flew to Montreal in the late afternoon.

"How do you like getting up every morning at five?" Lyle asked me.

Steve walked outside to check the coals in the tiny barbecue grill. I took his seat at the table.

"No big deal. I'm an early riser anyway, so it's not bad at all. Besides, I have the rest of the day to myself."

Paul emptied his bottle of beer. "You all talk about what a great company Mountain Air is," he said, rolling the empty bottle between the palms of his hands, "but you're flying charter while I'm still fueling planes. Instructing at Mountain Air won't be any better than anywhere else. In fact, it's probably worse because there are so few students. My prospects aren't promising after I get my instructor rating. Sometimes I think I'd be better off to go back to playing my tuba before I go too far with this flying stuff." Paul had been a promising musician in high school until he gave it up for airplanes.

"You probably play the tuba a hell of a lot better than you fly an airplane," Lyle jabbed, pushing his straight blond hair back off his forehead for it to fall right back. He was younger than Paul, but already an instructor.

Paul shot him a look and then glanced at me to see my reaction. "I just need to log hours by flying charters with you guys."

Steve came back in, and the screen door slammed behind him. He took the plate of hamburgers and hot dogs from the counter and went back out. I had already prepared all the other food for the evening—salad, corn, and brownies for dessert. Steve was taking care of the grill.

"Believe me, you don't know how good we have it here at Mountain Air until you've worked for a company like Cash Air," I said. "We had some fun in the beginning and got good flying time, but if you want to play by the rules, you're out."

"Or if you don't like airplanes that fall out of the sky," Lyle added.

"Yeah, I read all the articles about the crash." Paul looked at me seriously. The screen door slammed again. "What do you think happened to the guy who crashed?"

"Only Peter knows," I responded. "Peter and God."

Steve stood in front of us with a fresh bottle of beer. "Do we have to talk about that now?" He looked at me accusingly. "For just one night, I don't want to have to think about Cash Air."

His eyes had the cold look I had come to know so well, the attitude that always brought me down. I looked away, not giving in to it this time.

"What's the problem, Steve?" Pat asked him.

"There's no problem," he responded. "It was just a crappy situation I'd like to forget." He returned to the grill outside.

"Steve's one of the five pilots being investigated, isn't he?" Paul had read all the articles.

"He sure is, and he didn't tell Frank in the job interview," I said as I walked into the kitchen.

"Yeah, but Frank knows that some of the pilots are being scrutinized," I told them. "It didn't stop him from hiring us. There are no violations...yet."

The water for the corn was boiling, and I dropped the ears in one at a time, my face concealed by the steam rising from the pot. A hand on my shoulder startled me, and I spun to find Paul standing right behind me.

"What are you doing with him anyway?" he whispered. "I've been wondering since you came to Mountain Air."

I raised my eyebrows, surprised at his forwardness. We hardly knew each other. Now I knew others could see what a mismatch Steve and I were.

"I'd like to go out with you sometime," he continued boldly, still whispering so no one could hear, "if you can ever see your way out of his spell."

His words shocked me, and I looked to make sure Steve was still outside. "I've already promised myself that if Steve and I break up, there will never be another pilot in my life," I informed him with a half smile, enjoying the attention. "They don't make good dating material." I winked at him.

"If you break up? How about when you break up? That sounds like a healthier approach to Steve. I've noticed how he treats you." His voice was a little louder now.

"I've heard that before," I answered, not looking at him. I dropped the last ear of corn in the pot and opened the refrigerator to get the salad, hoping Paul would go back to the living room.

"If it helps," Paul persisted, "think of me as a musician rather than a pilot."

"Another beer?" I offered.

Paul shook his head.

"I'll have one," Steve interjected as he walked in from outside.

I handed him a bottle as he put the plate of grilled meat on the counter.

The phone rang. Steve went into the living room to answer it.

"Remember what I said," Paul reminded me and winked back.

I looked at him. It made me sad to think my life had declined to the point of living with someone others questioned, in a dirty apartment with no furniture and no comfort.

The call was from Frank. He assigned Pat a freight run for IBM that night, so we ate quickly, and they all left together in Paul's car.

"Want to go for a walk after we clean up?" I asked Steve.

Outside, it was still light, and now that they had left, the house was painfully quiet. The evenings we spent there depressed me. Steve was never much for conversation, and we did not have a television. It was better to have a late flight, or to stay in Burlington after an afternoon flight, but that wasn't always an option.

"No, I think I'll go to sleep early."

I looked at him from where I stood at the sink. "It's only seven thirty."

He paid no attention.

"Well, I need to get out of here for a little while. You sure you don't want to come?"

He was busy cleaning the small grill. "I'm tired. You can go yourself, you're a big girl."

I clenched my teeth as I stood over the dishes in the sink and scoured as hard as I could, shedding a few tears.

"I need the sink to rinse this off," he said, holding the grill with dirty hands.

"Alright, alright," I answered impatiently. I stopped scrubbing and moved aside to let him use the sink.

"What's your problem?" he asked me. "We had a good time tonight, at least I did, and now you look like you want to die. I can't figure you out. Cheer up!" He patted me on the back.

I rolled my eyes and walked away.

CHAPTER 23

Hornebrook

"Smile!"

I turned in my chair, and Mrs. Dunning's camera flashed in my eyes.

"I caught you off guard!" she exclaimed with delight. "That's the best kind of picture. We'll hang this one on the bulletin board with a caption below—Beth Ruggiero, Mountain Air's only female pilot as she prepares for a flight."

"Please don't do that," I pleaded, still smiling.

"Oh, don't be silly. We're very proud of you. Frank thinks the world of you, you know." Her exuberance was much loved by the employees at Mountain Air. "You and Steve both, in fact. Frank says Steve is such a talented pilot."

My smile disappeared.

"But, personally, I am thrilled we've got a lady pilot on board now," she said. "All through the years with Frank in the Air Force, living all over the world, there were so few ladies flying airplanes. Even now, there aren't so many."

"Did you ever learn to fly?" I asked.

"No, no. I'm content to let Francis do the flying. I go up with him occasionally. And I've taken the 'pinch hitter' course in case anything ever happens to him while we're in the air. But

I'm no pilot." She shook her head. "There was enough excitement when he went off to the wars, me at home wondering if he'd be coming back."

"Which wars did he serve in?"

"Well, we met during World War II, and when that was over, I was so thankful. But the Air Force was his career, and when the war in Korea began, he went there, too. And then there was Vietnam. He flew the fighters, and they needed him. Whether he was flying at war or at home, though, I never knew from day to day if I'd see him again. For all of us pilots' wives, it was the same. We learned to support each other."

"That must have been so difficult." I looked deeply at her trying to understand what she must have felt all those years.

"Yes," she said, her mind traveling back to other times. "I suppose it was, but I was younger then, and you can stand more when you're young like you are. And I prayed a lot. It saved me many times, especially when I saw another wife get news of her husband's death."

"I can't imagine what it's like to love someone so much that you can accept that risk each day of your life together."

"Sure you can," she replied. "Don't you and Steve take that risk for each other right here at Mountain Air?"

My eyes met hers. "No, it's not that way at all."

"Well, enough about that, Beth! You look so professional in your uniform. It will thrill the passengers to have such a pretty lady as their pilot."

I was wearing the gray wool pants and navy blazer Mrs. Dunning and I had shopped for the week before. It was my Mountain Air pilot uniform, to be worn when transporting passengers. And today, Sunday, was my first passenger flight.

"I won't bother you anymore," Mrs. Dunning said. "I can see you're trying to get ready, and the weather's not so good out there. Good luck, dear, you'll do just fine."

She walked back down the hall to the reception area, humming as she went. A minute later, I heard her talking to the fish in the tank. It was an ongoing conversation every time she passed the aquarium. She even had a name for each of them.

The weather was poor, similar to the days of instrument training with Steve. I was headed to Berlin, New Hampshire to pick up a group of passengers and bring them back to Burlington. The weather briefer at Flight Service informed me of a NOTAM in effect for the Berlin VOR—it was out of service. For that reason, only one instrument approach was available for Berlin, and that was the non-directional beacon, or NDB, approach: the one approach I never really liked. It wasn't what they called a precision approach like an ILS because NDBs were never, well, precise in where they dropped you after completing the approach. At small, uncontrolled airports, though, they were common, especially here in Vermont.

With the flight plan filed and the airplane pre-flighted, I started the engines on N600S—November-Six-Zero-Zero-Sierra, or Six-Hundred-Sierra for short. It was a Navajo Chieftain, much nicer than the ones I had flown at Cash Air. All the equipment was in working order in these planes, and the interiors were clean. And even though they were the same vintage as Ren's planes, they felt a lot newer.

The airport was quiet this afternoon as I rolled across the ramp and onto the taxiway. I allowed a light drizzle to accumulate on the windshield before turning on the windshield wiper.

"Six-Zero-Zero-Sierra, cleared for takeoff, fly runway heading," instructed the voice from the tower.

"Roger, Six-Hundred-Sierra, runway heading," I acknowledged and taxied onto the runway.

Once in the air, the ceiling was higher than reported, and it was not until eight hundred feet or so that I penetrated the clouds. The flight to Berlin was a short one, and on an instrument flight plan, it had to be flown the way the controllers dictated.

I was careful and judged every movement and maneuver as though it was a flight test. Frank had held me off from flying passengers until now.

I tuned the ADF on the right side of the instrument panel to Hornebrook, the NDB facility located on the ground at Berlin Airport. The Morse code identifier—HXK—was not audible, but the ADF tested fine, so I was probably still too far out for reception.

At approximately fifteen miles out, the Boston Center flight controller instructed, "Six-Zero-Zero-Sierra, you are cleared for the approach at Berlin. Contact Unicom and report on the ground at Berlin to close your flight plan." Berlin was an uncontrolled airport.

I switched to the Unicom frequency. "Berlin Unicom, Navajo Six-Zero-Zero-Sierra, inbound for the NDB approach, looking for airport advisories."

My call solicited only silence, so I tested the ADF again, this time successfully, and again listened for the Morse code identification, unsuccessfully. I continued on the heading last assigned by Boston. It was the general heading for the airport and for Hornebrook. Even if just the identifier portion of the NDB wasn't working, the needle on the gauge would point in the same direction I was flying, but the needle pointed to four o'clock. Without the signal, I could not do the approach, the only approach in service on the field. My stomach turned as I considered the possibility that my first passenger charter might be a failure.

"Berlin Unicom, Navajo Six-Hundred-Sierra, NDB approach, airport advisories please." I repeated my request with increasing irritation.

Still no answer.

"Berlin Unicom, Six-Hundred-Sierra, do you read?"

I was about to give up in disgust when a hole in the clouds gave me a clear view to the ground below. It was my only chance, and I pulled back the throttles and dove through the hole before it closed. I leveled in a scattered layer of clouds at eight hundred feet above the ground, letting out a sigh of relief when the airport came into view about three miles off the nose.

The landing was smooth and even twenty minutes ahead of the scheduled arrival time. The ramp was quiet and empty, and I parked in front of a maintenance hangar and shut the engines down. To the left was an office with a fuel truck parked in front. Since there had been no answer to my calls, I assumed the office would be locked, but a light inside showed otherwise. I stepped onto the ramp and walked across to the office. The door was open, and as I went in, a middle-aged man with tousled brown hair and a day-old beard looked up from the counter. He appeared to be doing accounting work in a ledger book.

"You work here?" I asked.

"Yup."

"I just flew in a minute ago."

"Yeah, I heard ya," he answered, looking back down at the ledger. His hair fell forward.

"I called in for advisories," I said. "Three times."

"I heard ya," he informed me without looking up.

"You heard me, and you didn't answer?"

"Yup."

I stared at him in disbelief as he continued to scribble on the paper. "You know," I said, "the NDB isn't listed in the NOTAMs as out of service. I think you need to call it in. There is no instrument approach to this airport right now."

"Hornebrook ain't out of service."

"What do you mean?"

"It ain't broke," he insisted, finally looking up at me.

"Yes, it is. I had no signal coming in, and my ADF tested fine."

He shrugged. "Don't matter. The thing ain't broke."

"Then how do you explain the lack of signal?"

He dragged the back of his hand under his nose. "Because it's not turned on."

"What?" My voice rose.

"You don't hear too well, do ya?"

"I don't think I'm the one with the hearing problem."

"If ya don't call ahead to let me know you're coming in," he said flatly, "then I don't turn it on."

"I just told you, I called in three times."

"You didn't call on the telephone. You pop up on Unicom and expect everything to be ready for you. It don't work like that here, and that's how I teach you damn pilots how it does work here."

The door opened, and three men walked in. I took a deep breath to compose myself and looked away from the crazy man in front of me.

"We're looking for someone from Mountain Air," one man said.

"Yes," I answered calmly. "It's that airplane right there."

The four passengers walked in single file to the Navajo on the ramp. I followed them and stood by the passenger door as each one stepped in. The last one stopped at the door and smiled at me.

"Are you coming, too?" he asked, trying to be friendly.

"I sure hope so—I'm the pilot."

His face turned red. "Oh," he laughed, "I thought the man inside was the pilot."

"Lucky for you," I informed him, "he's not."

CHAPTER 24

Stepping Back

By the end of the first month in Vermont, I bought my own futon and moved my belongings and myself to the second bedroom in the house. The atmosphere in the house was dismal, and since we had moved from Massachusetts, Steve was more distant than usual, with less and less to say. With little to talk about except our flight schedules, we had minimal conversation. There wasn't even a television to liven things up. I wasn't used to sharing my living space, and sharing it with Steve and his peculiar ways made it worse. Living with him made it painfully clear that Steve was just like his father.

Despite everything, some of the intimacy was intact. I thought I still loved him, and I knew I still needed him. But I found myself more and more consumed with depression, spiraling downward. Feelings of self-loathing defined my depression, different from any previous sadness I had felt. I kept it to myself, but it must have shown to some extent. By moving to the second bedroom, I was retreating like a wounded animal. By closing the door, I could lick my wounds.

It wasn't helping, though. Instead, I was alone to indulge self-destructive thoughts and contemplate ways to punish myself. At the same time, Steve's presence in the house seemed to ooze negative energy, and no bedroom door or wall could block it. It was like a black slime that found its way through every crevice and around every obstacle. After three weeks in my room, I resolved to find my own apartment in Burlington. I didn't tell Steve.

Within a few days of looking, I found a one-bedroom basement apartment and planned to move in on the weekend. Now I had to tell Steve.

"You're sure about this?" he asked when I told him that night. "You'll be paying more rent."

"I'm sure," I answered without trying to justify my decision.

The next morning, Steve left early for a flight, and I welcomed the chance to be alone to pack my clothes, my new futon, the green lamp and table, and my flight gear. I drove away from North Hero, never planning to return.

———

"I want to see you three times a week," the therapist said at the end of our first meeting. "I would also like to get you on anti-depression medication. How do you feel about that?"

Dr. Schlegel, or Dick, was a psychiatrist in town. I had found his name in the yellow pages.

"The only problem with the medication is my flying," I answered, "but if there is something with no side effects, please let's try it. I can't keep going like this without some help."

Dick nodded at my concern, and I hoped I had adequately conveyed the predicament. Thinking for a moment, he nodded slowly.

"There are very few choices, but I'd like to try putting you on lithium. It's a relatively benign drug in terms of side effects," he explained, "but I'm hoping it will help to lift you out of the ditch you're in and level things out. It's often used for bipolar disorder. I don't think you're bipolar, but I'd like to try it anyway." He walked to his desk for a prescription pad and wrote it out. "If you ever need to call in between appointments, this is my number. Don't hesitate."

I walked outside, where the sun was still bright, and felt a glimmer of hope. I strolled over to a public phone at the other end of the parking lot. I dug a dime out of my purse, inserted it, and dialed Steve's number. It rang three times.

"Hello," came the groggy answer.

"Steve, hi," I said. "Were you sleeping?"

"Uh huh."

"Oh, I'm sorry. I just wanted to see if you want to come over to my apartment tonight."

There was no answer.

"I'll make dinner for you," I offered.

"No, I'm picking up Joe at LaGuardia tomorrow morning."

I winced. Steve was Joe's favorite pilot and always handed him a fifty-dollar bill after a flight. The one time I had flown Joe, he didn't give me a tip. The flight was fine, smooth landing, but no tip.

The hope I felt a few moments ago had already evaporated.

"I guess I'll see you tomorrow."

"Right. I love you. Bye." He hung up.

I hung onto his words. They reassured me we were still together. Even though I had moved out, it was not because we had broken up. I was still clinging to the relationship.

CHAPTER 25

Back in Time

The road to Middlebury had a comforting familiarity. Dairy farms and general stores. White clapboard churches. Old and new tractors. All these things were just as they were when I was in college just a few years earlier, before airplanes entered my world. During those years, studying Chinese language and history filled my time along with a few boyfriends, and the biggest questions in my life were whether to go to graduate school or where to find a job.

The college soon appeared on the hill ahead along with memories of happy times. How had that life become so distant in such a short time? It didn't belong to me anymore. The recent months and events had painted my world black, in contrast to the college years.

Part of that past was Gregory Chiang, my Chinese professor. Patiently coaching his students, Gregory never showed the frustration he must have sometimes felt teaching his students the most difficult language in the world. He was in his forties and Chinese in most ways, American in a few others. His Chinese ways—the quiet patience and inner reserve—became clearer when I returned after studying abroad junior year in Taiwan.

Main Street in Middlebury was quiet, the shops just closing for the night. I turned toward Gregory's house, the same one he'd always had. The driveway was empty—he had no car—and I parked where I had many times before for parties and dinners he held for his students.

I knocked on the back door. The lights were on in the kitchen, and the smell of Chinese food drifted out as Gregory opened the door. I had forgotten how tall he was, taller than most Chinese because his ethnic roots were in Manchuria, a province in northern China.

"*Chiang Laoshi!*" I greeted him with a term of respect— *Teacher Chiang*—and a big smile.

"Hello, hello, it's good to see you." His face was the same, its calmness coming through with every word. There were no extremes of temperament, just an even, dependable calm.

We exchanged words in Chinese, which I had rarely used in the previous couple of years. It felt good to hear my voice say the words with much of the fluency I once had.

"How have you been?" I asked, our hands clasped together in a warm shake. "I've missed you."

"I'm fine. Nothing's changed. Do you miss Middlebury?"

"Much more now that I've come back. It brings back so many good memories."

We switched again to conversing in Chinese while we stood in the kitchen, and he told me the news of the college and other professors. His voice was distinctive, slightly high in pitch and a bit nasal. The sound of it returned me to his classroom.

The small table in the dining room was set with rice bowls and chopsticks. Gregory added the simple dishes he had pre-pared—eggs scrambled with tomato chunks, chicken with mushrooms and bamboo shoots.

"These smells take me right back to Taiwan," I said. "I've never stopped missing that place and my life there. Sometimes I have dreams I'm back in Taipei, and when I wake up, I spend my whole day thinking about going back."

He picked up his chopsticks to eat. "Why don't you go back?" he asked.

"Unless I change what I'm doing," I said, "I'll have no opportunity or reason to go back."

"Not if you get a job flying for China Airlines."

The idea intrigued me for a moment. "That would be great, but I don't think the Chinese in Taiwan will be hiring any female pilots in the near future. Besides, I'm a little down on flying these days. I don't know if it's worth it."

"It's only worth it if it makes you happy."

I nodded, thinking about what he said. "Usually it does, but sometimes it doesn't. I've been thinking about applying to graduate school." It was the first time I had revealed these private thoughts.

Gregory looked up with interest. "In what?"

"Chinese studies. At Tufts. I want to apply to the Fletcher School of Law and Diplomacy. In fact, I already have the application. I'd still fly, but it wouldn't be my career."

The application had arrived the week after moving into my new apartment, and I worked on it a little each day. I knew I could safely discuss it with Gregory. He was detached from my life at the same time as he was a familiar soul who never judged.

"Superb choice. You'll be a strong candidate. Can I do anything to help?"

"I'll need a letter of recommendation, and I'll be applying to come to the summer language school here at Middlebury," I confided. "My Chinese will need shaping up."

"I'm happy to hear this. It always surprised me you didn't pursue further studies."

I looked out the window, daylight fading. "I've been working toward a goal, Gregory. I want to fly for the airlines."

"Where did it come from?" he asked. "When you left here, you had a job taking tour groups to China, isn't that right?"

I nodded, recalling the excitement I had felt. I told him about leading my first tour and how it ended.

Gregory sat back in his seat and listened. When I finished, he poured more beer and brought out a dish of orange slices.

"Then how did you decide to start flying?" he asked.

"Well, I took time off to recover from the optic neuritis before going back to China with another group. At some point during that time, I remember sitting on the beach, and a small plane flew over. Nothing unusual, but that day it caught my attention. I watched it buzzing by and remembered one of my childhood goals to learn to fly. That's all it took. The way I really wanted to do it was in the Navy, but my medical history ended that."

I looked at him, perhaps hoping for some feedback, but he sat silently. Several minutes passed, and I finished my beer. Gregory refilled it.

"Do you have a boyfriend?"

The question made me squirm a little in my seat. "Yes, and that's the problem," I answered, surprising myself with the response. "He was my flight instructor, but the whole situation has taken me down. The fact is, though, I can't bring myself to just break it off."

"I thought you mentioned someone on the phone when you called the other day."

"Pilots don't make good boyfriends. Flying is more important to them than anything else."

It was late when I left Gregory's house, and I was tired from the beer and the talking. On the dark road back to Burlington, I thought about our conversation. Without many words, he had brought me back to a simpler time.

CHAPTER 26

New Year's Eve

"I'm sorry to call you in for a flight on New Year's Eve," Frank apologized from behind his desk. "But when IBM calls, we jump."

"Poughkeepsie again?" I asked.

"Yes. Only two boxes, so it's a light load. You can take someone with you for company if you'd like. Paul asked if he could go."

I crossed the hall to the pilots' room, where we prepared for our flights. Paul was already there waiting for me.

"Can I join you?" he asked with a grin, his dark hair dotted with damp spots from the snow that had begun falling.

"Sounds like you've already arranged it." I sat at the desk and opened my flight bag. "It's New Year's Eve. Don't you have a date or a party to go to?"

"Sure I do. Right here."

I shook my head, smiling. He knew I wasn't interested but enjoyed making me squirm a bit. "If flying boxes to Poughkeepsie on a snowy New Year's Eve is your idea of a date, Paul, then by all means you're welcome to join me. It'll be nice to have the company."

"Is that all I am to you? Company?" he said half joking-ly. "That's disappointing. Remember, Beth, think of me as a musician, not a pilot." He had a great smile and rarely was he not smiling.

"Then I have a date with a musician in an airplane, and we'll be back with plenty of time to go out."

"Yeah," he said, "but Steve will be there."

I glanced up at him from the desk. "Is the airplane fueled?"

"I don't know. Which one are we taking?"

"Bravo-Echo," I said, picking up the phone to call Flight Service. "Top all four tanks." Bravo-Echo was short for N555BE, an older Chieftain mainly used for freight flights.

By the time we were airborne, the snow was falling heavily. For the moment, though, it was a dry snow, and Flight Service told me it would probably taper off as we moved south toward our destination. The airplane was light with our load of two boxes, both strapped in the rear of the fuselage. It was a rou-tine flight that IBM requested almost daily from Burlington to their facility in Poughkeepsie, New York. Since my arrival at Mountain Air, IBM's need for freight flights had grown to about half the company's charter business. There were other destina-tions as well, such as Manassas, Virginia, but Poughkeepsie was the most frequent.

"Did you hear the rumor about California?" Paul asked me through the intercom, which was working well tonight for a change.

"No, what about it?"

"I don't know if it will really happen or not, but I over-heard Frank on the phone talking about a possible flight to California for IBM."

"Are you serious?" I exclaimed. "That can't be true."

"Well, Frank was talking to the people at IBM," he explained, "and there was a discussion of them needing a charter to San Francisco. If it happens, it would be the best flight anyone could hope for."

I tried to hold my excitement down. A flight across the country was something I had dreamed about since I had my private license. "A freight flight?" I asked.

"Has to be. IBM never sends passengers with us. And besides, why would you send passengers from Vermont to California in a Navajo? They'd send them on a corporate jet or at least first class on an airline for less money and more comfort."

"For that matter, they could put freight on an airline flight for a lot less money, and it would be a lot quicker," I puzzled. "Are you sure you heard right?"

"Yeah, his door was open, and he was on the phone for about half an hour discussing it with them. He didn't tell anyone about it after," Paul laughed. "Just kept us wondering."

"Who else heard him?"

"Steve."

"This is the first I've heard about it." It annoyed me that Steve had said nothing. "But then again, what difference does it make? Frank will go in order of seniority for that flight, which certainly doesn't put me in the running. Whoever gets it, though, is really lucky."

We flew across the line of the front well south of the Massachusetts border, and by the time we were ten miles from Poughkeepsie, an instrument approach was no longer needed. The skies were clear.

The courier was waiting for us and drove up in a van as soon as I shut down the engines. Fifteen minutes later, I had clearance for the second half of our flight back to Burlington, and we were airborne again.

"It looks like we'll be back by eight o'clock," I told Paul. "That's not too bad. Plenty of time to go out."

"So you'll be my date?" he asked.

I just smiled behind my microphone, feeling a little sad. Too bad I wasn't into Paul, and it couldn't be a real date. Steve had never shown as much interest in me.

"How much snow are they calling for?" he asked as we flew back into the clouds.

"Just a few inches."

By the time we were abeam Albany to the east, enough ice had collected on the wings to warrant inflating the boots.[9] It blew off in chunks, opaque ice that built up rapidly in these types of clouds. Already, a half inch of the white crust covered the windshield like a window shade. I turned on the switches for windshield and propeller heat to de-ice. The wings, though, needed constant attention. I inflated the boots at intervals when enough ice built up on the leading edges of the wings. It added interest to an otherwise routine flight. My experience with ice was limited to these past months in Vermont, where winter flying in icing conditions could always be expected.

"November-Five-Five-Bravo-Echo, Boston Center," the controller called for my attention.

"Roger, Boston Center," I replied.

"Five-Bravo-Echo, I need you to hold at the GRISS intersection. Hold on the airway, three-mile legs. Expect further clearance at zero-zero-four-five Zulu.[1]"

---

9   "Boots" are inflatable rubber membranes attached to the leading edge of each wing that, when inflated, expand to break up accumulated ice.

The controller immediately went on to another aircraft with similar holding instructions. Paul and I looked at each other with surprise, wondering what could possibly cause a delay into the tiny Burlington airport on New Year's Eve. Zero-zero-four-five Zulu was forty minutes away. Holding instructions were rare at the airports we flew into for Mountain Air. It was something that usually happened at the busy New York airports, not in Vermont.

I waited for a break in the radio communications and asked, "Boston Center, Five-Bravo-Echo, is there a problem at Burlington?"

"Roger, Five-Bravo-Echo, the airport is closed." He was busy, and his tone was terse, as if to tell me not to bother him with questions. *Just hold as instructed and leave me to do my job.*

"We're not getting any more information from him," I said to Paul and tuned the second radio to Burlington ATIS to listen to the recorded airport information:

BURLINGTON INTERNATIONAL
INFORMATION SIERRA. 1000 ZULU. AIRPORT
IS CLOSED UNTIL FURTHER NOTICE DUE
TO AIRCRAFT ACCIDENT. BURLINGTON
INTERNATIONAL INFORMATION SIERRA…

I turned it off. The ice was building rapidly on the airplane and needed my attention. After twenty-five quiet minutes in the racetrack holding pattern, I told Paul, "Tune in Burlington Approach and see if you can find anything out."

The icing was heavy and slowed us considerably, so fuel was lower than I wanted to see. Also, if there had been an accident at the airport, the delay could be much longer than forty minutes.

"Burlington Approach, Five-Five-Five-Bravo-Echo," Paul announced.

"Roger, Bravo-Echo," came the response. These controllers were familiar with each of Mountain Air's aircraft.

"We haven't been handed off to you yet," Paul began, "but we're holding near Glens Falls right now and are wondering if you could tell us how long you think the delay getting into Burlington will be."

"Roger, Bravo-Echo. There's been a crash on Runway 15. It will be a while. Consider going to your alternate."

"Roger."

For a moment, the only sound was the propellers winding their way out of sync. I put my hand on the throttles to adjust them.

"Five-Five-Bravo-Echo," said the voice of Boston Center. "Continue holding as previously instructed. Expect further clearance at zero-one-one-zero Zulu."

"Roger, continue holding," I confirmed and then turned to Paul, "This won't work. Our required reserve fuel was from Burlington to Plattsburgh as the alternate plus forty-five minutes beyond that. I took more than that, but we've already used the reserve and probably then some because of this ice. Check weather at our closest alternates and see which one is our best bet." I handed him the chart from my lap. "I'd rather not cross the lake to New York, so keep it in Vermont."

Paul went to work with the map and the second radio getting weather conditions at the nearest airports. After a few minutes, he reached into my flight bag for the binder of approach charts for the northeast. He thumbed through two or three times and then reached into the bag for another binder.

"Where are the Vermont charts?" he asked.

"Where they're supposed to be, in this binder." I reached over to the first one he had pulled from the bag. "All the New England states are in my number one binder."

"Well, Vermont's not here—OH SHIT!!" he swore. "I borrowed your Vermont and New York sections to make copies for myself while you were talking to Frank…"

I looked at him sharply, losing patience. "What are you telling me, Paul?"

"I forgot to put them back."

"Are you kidding me?"

"No," he said with a degree of shame. "I'm not kidding. But it wouldn't have been a problem if we were just going back to Burlington. You know those approaches by heart."

"Dammit, Paul, it's just not that simple. Look, if we're going to an alternate, there's not a whole lot of fuel to do it with. What have you found?"

He looked back down at the chart. "I think Montpelier is the best choice, but it's IFR there like everywhere else, and without approach charts, we can't do anything."

I thought quickly and urgently. "No, there is a way around this. Montpelier is the right choice. There's an ILS approach there, and that's all I need." I would tune in the frequency, fly assigned heading until intercept, and follow the course and glide slope down to two hundred or three hundred feet above the airport elevation. If all went as planned, the runway centerline would be aligned with the flight path. I took the map from him and glanced at the frequencies. "Boston Center, Five-Bravo-Echo," I called.

"Five-Bravo-Echo, go ahead."

"We'd like to change our destination to Montpelier."

"Roger," he replied. "Five-Five-Five-Bravo-Echo cleared to Montpelier via direct Montpelier at six thousand feet." After several minutes, the controller instructed, "Contact Boston Center on 135.7."

I read back his instructions and redialed the radio frequency. "Boston Center, Navajo Five-Five-Five-Bravo-Echo with you at six thousand feet. We'd like to request the ILS into Montpelier."

"Roger, Five-Bravo-Echo at six thousand feet," came the response. "The ILS at Montpelier is out of service. The VOR to runway three-five is in use."

"Fuck!!" I swore into the intercom. The only way I could blindly execute an instrument approach without the chart to guide me was to do an ILS, a precision approach, as opposed to the VOR, a non-precision approach. With the VOR approach, there was no instrument guidance for the glide slope—I needed a chart for the altitude stepdown instructions—and the VOR course guidance had nothing to do at all with the runway centerline. It would just drop us off in the airport's vicinity at a higher altitude and further out. Without the approach chart or familiarity with the airport, or without daylight and reasonably clear weather, it was a shot in the dark.

I tuned in the VOR frequency of 110.8 and listened for the Morse code identifier…dash-dash-dot-dash-dash-dot-dot-dot-dot-dash…"At least we have something reliable there," I said disgustedly. "If the ceiling there is one thousand feet, as you said, then hopefully this'll work."

"That was the last report." Paul's voice was timid, knowing he had messed up.

I hit the switch to inflate the boots. "The biggest problem I see with this is we don't know the exact radial to fly off the VOR when we hit it. It's for Runway 35, so I'll fly the 350-degree radial, but that could be ten or even twenty degrees off. That makes me nervous with the hills around here. I need you to look for the airport lights."

"Okay," he said, relieved to have an assignment. "No sweat, it's gonna be fine."

"That's how I used to feel when I sat in that seat. Wait till you're in my seat. You'll be sweating plenty then."

"Five-Bravo-Echo," the controller called, "descend to four thousand feet. Cleared for the VOR approach to Runway 35 at Montpelier. Contact Unicom. Call Flight Service on the ground to close out your flight plan."

I brought the power back and descended quickly to the assigned altitude. The Distance Measuring Equipment showed we were three miles from the VOR. If all went smoothly, the fuel would not be an issue at all.

"I just hope that Boston Center isn't watching our flight path and wondering what the hell we're doing," I mumbled into the intercom. "Without a chart, I'm doing a straight-in approach. No procedure turns."

Paul called Montpelier Unicom with no success. "What's going on here? No one's answering."

"It's New Year's Eve. What do you expect?"

He grumbled and turned his attention outside. "How am I supposed to do the looking for the airport if you don't turn on the windshield deicer?"

I looked at the windshield still coated with white ice and checked the deicer switch. It was on. No popped circuit breakers either.

"Damned thing picked a hell of a time to break," I cursed. "This sucks. I have no approach plate, and we can't even look for the airport. It's IFR and snowing, and there are mountains on all sides of this friggin' airport."

"We're screwed," Paul whined.

"You could say we'll just be incredibly lucky if we get to see the New Year come in tonight."

The flag flipped on the VOR as we crossed over it. I turned course to intercept the 350-degree radial. From here, it was guesswork, and hopefully a lot of luck.

"I think the airport is about eight or nine miles from the VOR," I said as I brought the power back for descent. "Maybe a little less. What's the airport elevation?"

Paul didn't answer. I looked over and saw a vacant look on his face.

"Look on the chart," I yelled, "don't go blank on me now! I need your help here. Montpelier is where you learned to fly. Find the damn airport!" We might not have the instrument approach plate to give us the necessary landing instructions, but at least with the VFR chart we would know what ground references to look for. If only we could see them.

He fumbled with the VFR chart. "It's, uh, 1,165."

"Okay," I said, right hand on the throttles, "we're a half mile from the VOR now. I'm going to descend to two thousand so there'll be as much time as possible to find the airport and pray there aren't any hills in the way."

"How are we going to find it?" he whined again. "You can't see shit through this ice."

"I'll fly sideways, S-turns and slips. You look out the side window."

At two thousand feet, we were two-and-a-half miles from the VOR and still in the soup. I inflated the boots and three quarters of an inch flew off. "Keep hitting the deicer switch for the windshield while you're looking outside," I told him. "Maybe we'll get lucky."

"You're through!" he shouted. "I can see the ground!"

We were at eighteen hundred feet above sea level, just seven hundred feet above ground level at the airport.

"It's a lot lower than I hoped. Montpelier sits in a valley. There are a lot of hills higher than us."

"Yes."

"Alright, I will have to stay strictly on this radial, and hopefully the prescribed radial on the approach plate I don't have isn't much different."

I began S-turns on the course, and we took turns looking out the side windows through the falling snow. Runway lights were pilot controlled, and I turned them to their highest intensity with seven clicks of the microphone. At eight miles from the VOR, there was still no sign of the airport. The glimpses out the side windows were barely a few seconds long each, not nearly enough to locate a small airport in bad visibility. My heart was pounding.

"We're nine miles from the VOR. It's got to be close," I said. I did one more turn to the right and took a hard look outside. Nothing but darkness. "Dammit! I'm turning around and backtracking to the VOR. We'll try another scan."

"Why don't we try somewhere else?" he asked plaintively.

"You don't get it, do you? Have you looked at our fuel lately? There isn't enough to go anywhere else. The ice has been bogging us down for the past hour and a half. Not to mention we have no approach plates."

At six miles from the VOR, now heading back toward it, I still didn't see the airport lights. I began a turn back again and changed the course by ten degrees, believing we must be on the wrong radial.

"What are you doing?" Paul asked as we turned.

"It's around here, either left or right of us," I explained, "so I'll circle until we find it. I've got to keep the turn tight."

Twice around to the left, and there still was no sign. On the third time around to the right, Paul yelled, "There it is! Right over there!"

I leveled the wings, and he pointed to about one o'clock off the nose. I turned hard to the right so I could see it off the left wing. There it was, about two miles out. I memorized its location because after the turn was complete, the icy windshield would again obscure the view. After a minute, the airport reappeared directly ahead of us as we crossed Runway 35.

"We can't afford to lose sight of the runway," I warned. We crossed the runway, and I turned tightly to parallel it closely. "This will be a low, close pattern, so be prepared for a steep turn."

Abeam the runway numbers and not wanting to go much further for fear of losing it in this blind approach, I banked the wings forty-five degrees. Any ice on the wings could be disastrous in a steep turn, but I would have to sweat it all the way around the 180 degree turn to line up on short final.

Halfway through the turn, Paul panicked. "What're you doing?" he yelled and grabbed the controls, putting the plane in an even steeper bank. Before I could grab it back from him, we were at a near stall, nose up.

"Let go!" I screamed at him. "Let go!" I threw my right arm across his chest with a force I didn't know I had. It stunned him, and with both hands I wrestled the controls back under my power. Paul let go in a daze. He had nearly botched the approach, but I resolved not to lose it. I stuffed the nose down to a safe attitude and finished the turn to line up with the runway. It was slipping behind us with every second. With only the runway lights as my guide, I touched down too fast and too long.

The layer of snow cushioned the touchdown, but the plane slid on the runway surface for the rest of its length. In those few seconds, I was sure crashing off the end was the only way we would stop.

But there was no crash as we came to a stop, still on the runway. The last runway lights glowed at my wing tip. I reached up and shut down the engines right there on the runway. My heart was racing hard and fast. I looked at Paul.

"I'm sorry," he mumbled. "I don't know what happened."

I opened the pilot's door and climbed out. "I want to see how much runway is left."

He followed me out, and together we looked at the Navajo's nosewheel just inches short of the end of the pavement. The only sound in the dark was our breathing, heavy with fear. For several minutes, we stood in the snow, silent and numb. I was thankful for having what it took to take control of what could have been a disastrous scene.

CHAPTER 27

Ready to Party

The airport terminal was empty, just one light left on for anyone who was passing through. Even the restaurant was dark. Paul and I sat alone waiting for Steve and Lyle to pick us up. They had been expecting our phone call after they heard news of the crash at Burlington.

"We're in Montpelier," I told Steve when he answered the phone in North Hero. "Burlington was closed. There was an accident."

"I know. It's still closed," he updated me. "It's been on the news all night."

It relieved me to know it was still closed. Getting back into that airplane tonight was unthinkable. Besides, there wasn't enough fuel and none here at Montpelier until tomorrow or the next day.

"Anyone we know?" I asked him.

"No, it was a family of five coming up from New York in a Cherokee Six to go skiing. The father was the pilot. It seems he told the controller earlier on he had iced up badly. They stalled on short final. Crashed and burned. It killed everyone except the youngest child."

I cringed. When I told Paul about it, I could tell he realized we could have had the same kind of stall if I hadn't been able to take the controls from him. We slumped down in the black vinyl seats.

"You okay?" he asked me.

"Except for the adrenaline overdose. You?"

"Embarrassed more than anything else. I can't believe I did that. Are you pissed?"

"I would have been if something bad happened," I answered. "We were lucky."

"You can't really blame me, you know," he continued. "I told you I was a musician and not a pilot."

"Well, I hope you're a better tuba player than a pilot." I shook my head, unable to laugh. For a long while we said nothing.

"Do you really think it was just luck?" He broke the silence.

"Either that or brute strength on my part."

Another pause.

"Do you ever feel that someone is watching over you?" he asked.

"Yes." I knew my father was right by my side.

Paul looked at me, surprised at the simple certainty of my answer. "Hmm," he mumbled and fell back into thought.

After a few minutes, I could hear Lyle's voice in the hallway. "Hey! Are you two ready for a party or what?"

I hadn't heard the car drive up, so his arrival startled me. Steve was close behind.

"Bad night?" Steve asked. He appeared out of the dark hallway and stood in front of us.

"How can you tell?" I responded without looking at him.

"You both look a little frazzled. Did you have any trouble?"

"You could say that," Paul volunteered.

Steve and Lyle looked questioningly at us, still slumped in the vinyl seats, waiting for an explanation.

"Come with me," I stood up and said, "I'll show you."

They followed us out to the ramp where Bravo-Echo sat in her sad state of deep freeze, snow accumulating quickly on the surfaces. "It started with an hour of holding over Glens Falls, heavy icing, and ended with low fuel and a VOR approach into here with this." I pointed up to the ice-covered windshield. I left out the other details of the flight, and Paul's face showed relief. He added nothing.

"Windshield deice broke?" Lyle asked.

"It sure did," I answered him.

Steve walked around the wings and tail observing the coat of ice. He said nothing. The crash at Burlington was ample evidence of the severity of the icing. Bravo-Echo's condition reinforced that. When he came around to where we stood, he put his arm around my shoulder and pulled me close. "You did have a tough night, didn't you?"

I put my head on his shoulder to enjoy the moment of compassion. He let his arm down and gave me a pat on the back. "Come on," he offered, "you could use a few drinks, maybe more."

CHAPTER 28

So Alone

I started dialing my therapist's phone number again after several false starts. He had told me to call him anytime I needed to talk, and this was the first time I was taking him up on it.

The phone rang only once before he answered.

"Dick, it's Beth."

"Yes, Beth," he replied. "What's going on?" His tone was reassuring.

"Well, Steve just told me Frank chose him to do the flight to California," I reported. He already knew this would probably happen through our previous sessions. "He leaves in two days."

"You knew it would most likely happen this way, Beth," he reminded me. "They hired him before you, right?"

"Yeah, but don't forget why they hired him before me, Dick." I reminded him impatiently. "It should have been me going to California if I hadn't told him about the interview."

"Are you upset because you'll miss him or you're jealous?"

I thought for a moment. "Mostly jealous," I acknowledged both to him and myself. "But I'll miss him, too."

"I would say that's progress," he said. "If you told me it was just because you'd miss him, I would be concerned. The fact that you're jealous is a healthier reaction than missing him."

Before our conversation ended, Dick asked, "Are you still following through with your grad school application?"

"Yes, I sent it," I replied with satisfaction.

"Well, that's something you've done alone. You should be proud."

"But that's just the application process," I responded. "The true test will come if I get accepted. Will I be able to follow through with it and enroll, leaving this life and my airline dreams behind?"

"When will you know?"

"About six weeks."

The phone call went as our sessions did, with me pouring out, and Dick listening and giving me alternative ways of thinking about it. When we hung up, I felt a little better but looked forward to our next visit. I depended on my visits with Dick more and more, now three times a week.

We both knew the lithium pills did nothing for my depression, but I continued to take them. He added a prescription for a tranquilizer, to be taken as needed when I wouldn't be flying. Still, it was a temporary fix, and there was always a next time, never an end to it all. Ironically, the visits to Dick were also something I did alone. It was my secret from the beginning, and it stayed that way.

CHAPTER 29

Heading West

There were days when I could glimpse my yet distant, but surely coming, emergence from this mire. Often, though, I would fall back, and the glimpse was far removed.

One such hopeful day came at the beginning of February 1988 while the snow fell heavily from dense clouds. The phone rang early in the morning from its place on the living room floor. Only a chair and a small television occupied that room, so the phone stayed on the floor. I crawled out from under the covers and stumbled into the cold air to the living room.

I answered groggily. This early, I felt entitled not to clear my throat and speak clearly.

"Hi Beth. Frank Dunning here." He sounded as if he'd been up for hours. "Sorry to bother you so early, but I think you'll understand when I tell you why."

"No bother, Frank," I said politely.

"I'm in the office now. Been here since three o'clock," he explained.

"Did something happen?"

"No, no," he reassured me. "IBM woke me up at home. They need another flight to San Francisco. You're next in line for that, you know, and I was sure you'd want to go."

I was fully awake now, the excitement surging as I stood up.

"I'll need you to leave today," he instructed. "Same thing as the other flight—fly out to San Francisco empty in Two-Five-Echo, meet the courier and pick up the box, fly the box to Lexington, Kentucky. Very simple. Lyle will go with you as copilot. You'll meet Steve and Paul out there, and the four of you will fly back to Kentucky together with the box. The airplane they flew out there will stay because IBM said they'd need one more box taken to Kentucky next week. I'll fly out there commercially and do that one myself when they need it."

"Okay!" I responded. "I'll get ready and meet you at the airport. You still don't know what's in the boxes?"

"Nope, no idea," he answered without speculation. IBM was paying over 25,000 dollars for each of these flights without a second thought. For that price, Frank didn't care what was in the box. He and all the other employees knew small charter companies only dreamed of such a customer. "Make sure you pack for a few nights," he added before hanging up.

"Yes!" I shouted after hanging up. "Yes!"

Smiling till it hurt, I did a dance around the living room and into the shower. The trip to California was the flight I had been dreaming of. Sitting in the lounge at New England Flyers after the students had gone home and the airplanes were fueled, we fantasized about doing it in the Cub, hoped that we could do it in any airplane, and despaired we might never get to do it. This was not Vermont to California in an airliner at 35,000 feet with a vague view of the Grand Canyon off the left wing. This was low-level flying, over whatever course I chose, stopping at whichever airports I wanted, seeing the country from above. And I was being paid to do it.

Now I would have the chance to match Steve on this flight of flights. He had called me two nights earlier when he and Paul arrived in San Francisco with details of the trip, making me so jealous I could not sleep.

"The best part was over the Rocky Mountains," he said after assuring me I had not lived until I did such a flight. He even suggested I rent an airplane sometime to fly the same route so I would not miss out on the wonderful experience. "When we climbed to get over the mountains, we kept going to see how high we could climb. We climbed 24,300 feet! I think we may have set a Navajo record for altitude. I'm going to call Piper when I get home and find out."

I packed my charts to do the evening run to Montreal, for which I was already running late. There would be no altitude records on the way to Montreal in the old Aztec. When Lyle and I arrived in San Francisco, it would be the first time seeing Steve since that phone call, and my goal was to break his Navajo altitude record on our way out there.

It was not until early afternoon that we were ready to take off from Burlington in the Navajo. We were delayed getting the oxygen system charged for the second half of the flight over the mountains. Lyle stayed with the airplane while I went to a nearby deli to buy sandwiches for the trip. I returned with two roast beef grinders, two orders of lasagna in Styrofoam containers, six bags of chips, and two bags of chocolate chip cookies.

"What's with all this food?" Lyle asked.

"Just making sure we have enough for that long climb to 25,000 feet," I answered. "We need two things for that—food and oxygen."

He smiled, knowing my intent.

By the time we left, snow covered the runway. We rolled down the slippery surface and took off into the clouds. It was IFR east of the Great Lakes and all the way beyond Buffalo where the clouds thinned. It didn't matter if the clouds obscured the ground. This area was of less interest than what was to come. I flew over different parts of it daily. Lyle and I flew patiently through the clouds and snow in anticipation of what we would see beyond. As though we were about to explore the unexplored, we waited in reverent silence to cross the imaginary line that divided our old world and the new world.

When we crossed that line west of Buffalo, though, it was already dark. Our first stop for fuel came in the late afternoon at South Bend, Indiana. Near Chicago, where the nighttime Cash Air flights had originated, I resigned myself to the fact that, once again, I would not be seeing this part of the country in daylight. At least not this time. Omaha would be the final destination for the night, leaving the best part of the trip for the next day.

The FBO[10] in Omaha was magnificent. They didn't build them like this in the Northeast, mostly because space was tighter, airports were older and smaller, and so were the FBOs. Out west, there was endless land to spread out on, and spread out they did. The main building was unmistakably new as were the hangars that extended from it. It would have taken ten minutes to walk from our parking spot on the enormous, newly paved ramp if the lineman who directed us there didn't have a golf cart.

We stepped out of the Navajo into the frigid cold. Wind whipped mercilessly across the ramp as Lyle and I hurried to take what we needed for the night. The lineman waited patiently for us.

---

10 An FBO, or fixed base operator, is an airport facility for servicing general aviation pilots and aircraft.

"We'll need full fuel for tomorrow morning, six o'clock," I instructed him. "Make sure it's one hundred low lead, not jet fuel. It's not a jet." At a place like this, they were accustomed to fueling corporate jets, and a disastrous mistake like jet fuel in a piston aircraft would be easy to make. "We'll also need a pre-heat tomorrow morning before we go."

The golf cart sped us across the ramp to the main building, aglow with lights and glass and corporate pilots, coming in and leaving in their jets, some even heading overseas. I couldn't help being excited—this was as close to my ultimate dream of flying jets as I'd been. Thoughts of graduate school suddenly paled compared to this world, and it reignited my spark for a career with the airlines.

In the warmth of the lobby, I gave my aircraft information to the man at the desk. It was a different world of flying out here, where pilots spoke with Southern accents or Midwestern twangs, and the bellies of short men grew larger and their hair thinner with each year of sitting in the cockpit, airport lounges, and hotel rooms. It was a world where the egos of many pilots expanded at unnatural rates to match the size or speed of the equipment they flew. Some strutted uncomfortably about the lounge when a female pilot entered their domain. For those who believed their male anatomy was the key to success in the cockpit, a woman's presence was a threat and a bother. To that kind of guy, women pilots were "honey" and "sweetheart," a small attempt on their part to regain lost ground.

———

Eight solid hours in flight, all of it either in IFR conditions or at night mostly over unfamiliar terrain, left us exhausted, and a clean bed in a nearby hotel was our only desire. We shared a room and awoke the next morning to clear skies and even colder temperatures.

Back out on the ramp, the lineman on duty preheated the engines while Lyle and I pre-flighted the airplane. Moving quickly to get off the cold ramp and into the slightly less cold airplane, we were efficient with no need for words. Even Vermont's winters seemed more tolerable than this.

Lyle climbed up the stairs and through the door, closing it behind him. "Where are we going first, Captain?"

"We're heading west, young man. Let's see how far the fuel takes us."

"Over the Rockies for the altitude challenge?" he asked.

"No. Poor weather in Colorado and north. Heavy snow. We'll head toward New Mexico, and after that the Grand Canyon. That's where the sun is shining. I've been waiting for this opportunity."

"What about breaking Steve's record?"

"We'll do it over the Sierra Nevadas. Not only that, if we went over the Rockies, we'd miss the Grand Canyon."

The cold no longer mattered as we anticipated our flight. The first track would be southwesterly with temperatures steadily rising. In Omaha, we were on the edge of the landscape we longed to see.

Omaha and its airport sit on the west side of the Missouri River. Because we landed in the dark the night before, we saw the river for the first time as we took off. Extending far into the horizon was another river running in a perpendicular direction. Lyle identified it from the chart as the Platte River.

From South Bend to Omaha in the dark, we had navigated from VOR to VOR, but this second day, we would meander in directions taking us to the sights we wanted to see. With this in mind, our first jog took us directly west along the path of the Platte River at two thousand feet.

Its bends and turns barely showed on the chart where it appeared as a straight line across the state of Nebraska. But rivers rarely run in a straight line—they snake through the terrain, winding around rocks and islands, and always end up where they aimed from the beginning. The scale of the map has no room for the patient process of a river's flow and therefore does it a great injustice. The only accurate prediction about a river is that it will reach its destination. How it gets there changes from mile to mile.

We were treated to a dramatic display of this over the next 120 nautical miles of the Platte. Just beyond Grand Island, Nebraska, we broke off from the river. Several smaller rivers passed below as we moved on to cut across the northwest corner of Kansas. They mainly ran in an east-west direction, creating a complicated maze the further they went. Ahead, the terrain rose higher, and our charts reflected it as the color on the paper shifted from light blue-green covering the eastern part of the country all the way to western Kansas. The new color assigned by the FAA was light beige as the ground rose from three and four thousand feet to five and six thousand feet above sea level. Below, the land itself was brown if not snow covered, showing less snow as our flight path gradually took us south. We crossed the great divider, Interstate 70, the road leading people from east to west and back east again, and soon reached the junction of Kansas, Colorado, and Oklahoma.

Kansas was now behind us. We flew over the southeast corner of Colorado and passed into New Mexico. Lyle unfolded the next chart, and the blue-green beige of the last chart disappeared. A steady darkening of the beige became brown. The terrain rose even more quickly now, and the earth bulged with hills and mountains. The snow disappeared, and the ground showed more brown than green. We followed Interstate 25 south from Wagon Mound, New Mexico to our first destination of the day—Las Vegas, New Mexico. We had decided the following stop after this would be Las Vegas, Nevada, so this choice seemed fitting. Besides, we had already taken the fuel to its limits for this leg of the journey.

Las Vegas, New Mexico was an oasis in a sea of browns. Green, quiet, and, from the ground, the biggest, bluest sky I had ever seen. There was a lake by the airport, just as blue as the sky above. Perhaps it was the quiet now that the engines were shut down, or perhaps it was just the natural quiet of this place that impressed me as I looked west at the Sangre de Cristo Mountains. Whatever the reason, the feeling of calm during that short moment on the ground was unforgettable.

The airport elevation neared seven thousand feet above sea level, almost two thousand feet higher than Denver. The air was thin and warm, and, after only a short break, we took off again. The runway was 7,900 feet long, extensive for a small airport, but thanks to the high elevation and the warm temperature even in February, the airplane labored slowly to get off the ground. Finally airborne, it was a lethargic climb to 12,000 feet, continuing west in close range of the Sangre de Cristos.

The contours of the earth spread out below inspired more awe with each passing mile. What had only been a paper depiction of the real thing back in the flight prep room in Burlington now came to life on the ground below. I appreciated that it would be magnificent but didn't imagine this.

According to the map, Indian reservations lay below and ahead. From the sky, you could distinguish reservations by the undeveloped land, with some farmland and lack of buildings within their boundaries. It seemed New Mexico existed solely for that purpose. Apache, Zuni, and then, after crossing the Continental Divide, the biggest one of all, the Navajo Nation. From above, it was endless miles of desert with few roads and people. We tracked to the Zuni VOR, and as we crossed it, the large white cone stood out on the sand like a misdirected torpedo in the blazing sun.

From Zuni, we tracked to Winslow, Arizona, and for most of that, the land remained untouched. Winslow was small, but the crater just west of it was not. About 50,000 years ago, a giant meteor collided with what is now the Arizona desert, leaving a pock mark lasting eons. We circled over it four times before turning northwest toward the Grand Canyon VOR.

In a short time, the desert took on a new, almost unreal appearance. It was the Painted Desert. I pulled power back to descend lower for a better view. Like a painter's palette, beautiful pastel colors from deep reds and lavender to orange and pink tones were dappled across the hills. I flew low and slow to take it all in.

After that, the most distinctive landmarks noted on the charts were not cities and towns, or even villages or individual buildings, but mines identified by vast sections of excavated earth. Further north, an occasional ranch or corral broke up the vastness.

When the Grand Canyon finally showed itself through the windshield at the end of the Painted Desert, a reverent hush replaced our oohs and aahs. Even though we had seen photographs, either of us had imagined the majesty of this canyon. The temptation was to dip down below the canyon's rim for a closer view, but just the year before a sightseeing flight below the rim had crashed into the side of the canyon, killing all aboard. Special aviation regulations went into effect soon after, and the FAA prohibited low flight. Even at five hundred feet above the rim, we were in violation of the new regulations, but we continued to follow the path of the Colorado River at that altitude. It was the finest example of what a river can do when it sets out for a destination.

It spilled into Lake Mead at the Nevada border, just short of our next fuel stop. The lake reached out in finger-like projections searching for the lowest ground it could find, and the longest of those projections was the Colorado River. Here was a beautiful body of water in the desert, a true oasis. Not until we passed Hoover Dam and Lake Mead was behind us did Las Vegas appear in its valley, and the oasis turned into a city.

The temperature in Vegas was just over sixty degrees, and we stayed only long enough to fuel and use the bathrooms, dropping a few quarters into the slot machines along the way. The machines lined the walls from the entrance, through the terminal, and into the bathrooms. We came out a few dollars poorer and taxied out to the runway for takeoff to an attempted altitude record.

Las Vegas sits in a bowl at an elevation of 2,500 feet above sea level, surrounded by mountains six thousand feet higher. Takeoff required circling to gain enough altitude to clear the mountains. We crossed to the west still climbing over the desert. Ahead lay the Sierra Nevadas, shown in the darkest brown contours on the map. Along our path, they would top out at close to 15,000 feet. We continued the climb, slowly mounting our way to the limits of the Navajo.

The Navajo's engines are turbocharged, not normally aspirated, so higher altitudes are within its capabilities. But they are not turbines—i.e., jets—and therefore have limits.

At 20,000 feet, we flew above Death Valley, a blue-green strip amidst the browns on the chart. The tiny Death Valley airport appeared far below us at 211 feet below sea level. We continued to climb. At 21,000 feet, it slowed to two hundred feet per minute, and we hooked up our oxygen masks. Lack of oxygen does the same things to the engines as it does to the body; they become sluggish and temperamental. With three thousand feet still to go to beat Steve's alleged record, it seemed it might not happen.

"They had the advantage of flying a Chieftain on their climb," I said disgustedly. "We're stuck with this older Navajo, and it doesn't perform as well."

The climb slowed to sixty feet per minute. I adjusted the throttles, props, and mixtures to keep it in the climb. The props surged, out of sync the whole way up. As soon as I corrected them, they went right back out of sync. Lyle and I sucked on oxygen the entire way up, and the engines wished they were, too.

"Give up?" Lyle probed.

"No way," I said. "We're getting there, slow but sure. Fifty feet per minute now." After twenty-five minutes, we went through 24,000 feet. "Three hundred more and we've got them beat. A thousand more, and we've made our goal."

"Your goal," he replied pointedly.

"Okay, my goal, but you're on board with this challenge, too."

As I crossed Steve's threshold, a satisfied, quiet smile fixed itself on my face and did not leave. Thirty minutes later, by the tramway at Owens Lake, the Navajo peaked at 25,000 feet, huffing and puffing all the way, props badly out of sync, and the throttles temperamental. We leveled there. My smile turned to a big grin and lasted all the way back down.

"We did it!" I announced triumphantly.

"Are you going to tell Steve as soon as you see him?" Lyle asked as we made our descent from the record 25,000 feet. Now that we had done it, he was as satisfied as I was.

"No, *you're* going to tell him," I answered.

"Why?" It surprised him. "It's your moment to get one up on Steve."

"If I tell him, he'll get that attitude on his face. If you tell him, he won't."

Lyle agreed.

"Satisfied?"

"Very."

CHAPTER 30

Almost There

"More sake," Steve told the tiny waitress dressed in an orange kimono. She smiled and nodded, as if acknowledging our increasing state of inebriation. "Make it two bottles," he added.

She smiled and nodded again.

The sushi and sashimi came in stages, at all times accompanied by warm sake. The alcohol took hold, fueled by the thrill of being in San Francisco with two airplanes, a couple of free days, and a company expense account.

"You missed a lot not going over the Grand Canyon," I told Steve and Paul, sitting across the table. "What a flight! We could go over it on the way back east," I suggested as I used my chopsticks to mix the soy sauce with wasabi in the tiny saucers.

"Yeah, but we won't see it," Steve said. He threw a shot of sake to the back of this throat. "We leave at night, day after tomorrow. It doesn't matter. There'll be other chances to fly over the Grand Canyon. Lots of other chances."

"Not with the airlines, if that's what you mean," Lyle said. "At least not for Paul."

"Of course with the airlines," Paul defended. "I'll see the best of this country and plenty of others, too."

"Except you'll be waiting a hell of a long time for that to happen," Lyle burst his bubble and then turned to Steve and me. "Maybe we'd better take a detour so Paul can see it. At the rate he's going, he'll be forty years old before he makes it to the airlines." Paul's total flying hours were only about five hundred, far short of having a career.

Paul gave Lyle a disgusted look. "The only one here who will make it to the airlines anytime soon is Steve," he shot back, winking at me. He always told me I would go faster and further than Steve, and I always responded that he was flattering me. Based on hard data, though—flying hours—Steve had the edge.

"I wouldn't be so sure of that," Steve said. "Not with the violation the Feds have hanging over my head."

"The hazmat flight for Cash Air?" Lyle asked.

Steve picked a spicy tuna hand roll and held it in front of his mouth. "What else?" he said and took a bite. "And it could take another year or more before they have a hearing and make a ruling. I'm screwed no matter how you look at it. The only way I'll be finding my way into a major airline soon is if the demand for pilots way exceeds the supply."

"And that is exactly what's happening now," Lyle added. "The airlines are hiring like crazy."

"Even if that doesn't happen," I said to Steve, "You could probably get a job with a commuter airline for a year and then transition to the majors. Then you'd have a track record."

Steve was getting agitated. "I'm not interested in flying for a commuter," he answered with disgust. "I can make more money flying Part 135 charters than with a scheduled commuter."

"True, but it probably won't get you to the airlines as fast," I responded.

"Have you heard what they pay pilots at that commuter airline in New Hampshire?" Paul interjected.

Steve looked at him.

"The starting pay is a hundred and fifty dollars a week. That's it. Less than you make working for Mountain Air. It's hardly better than a minimum wage job."

Four cups of sake were raised as we agreed on our disgust.

"I have to agree with Steve," I said. "It's better if you can skip the commuters and go straight to a major airline. I don't know if I'll be able to, but I'm sure going to try." Brief thoughts of graduate school crossed my mind as I said the words. "But Paul's right about you, Steve. You'll be the first to make it to the majors of all of us. I've only got about seventeen hundred hours logged at this point. You're at what? Almost three thousand?"

He nodded.

"And if you don't get to the airlines, who cares anyway?" I dropped my fist on the table, and the dishes rattled. "You can't see much of the Grand Canyon from 30,000 feet!"

Paul raised his cup again. "Let's have a toast. To our careers in flying and not being able to see much of the Grand Canyon from 30,000 feet. That we'll all make it to the majors by..." he paused, "...by the end of next year."

We laughed at the ridiculousness of such a hope but tapped the four cups together anyway and emptied the warm sake down our throats hoping it might come true.

Lyle quickly refilled our cups and raised his again. "I have a toast," he said. "To altitude records in Navajos. At 25,000 feet, gentlemen, you've been beat!"

I winked at Lyle, smiled with satisfaction and enjoyed the look of surprise on Steve's face. It was the first they learned of it, and I savored the moment, grateful that Lyle had been the one to announce it. After a moment, Steve just raised his eyebrows as if to say, "Whatever."

CHAPTER 31

Cancelled Plans

A nurse wearing tight polyester scrubs showed me to the phone. She had a kind face with warm eyes and a smile at the end of every sentence. It was comforting and helped me to forget momentarily why I was at the hospital, but the throbbing pain in my back reminded me.

My car was surely totaled. My weekend trip to Massachusetts to visit my mother had ended without having even left Burlington. The day was half gone, and I had no transportation, not even from the hospital where I now found myself.

I followed the nurse through the corridors of the emergency area, busy with the injuries that people are prone to on a sunny Saturday. They all looked unhappy, and I supposed I looked no different.

At the next left turn, there was a line of public phones. The nurse turned to leave. "Get some rest," she advised, "and call if you have any problems. The doctors won't tell you this, but what you need for that injury is a good chiropractor."

"Thank you," I said and picked up a phone. I dialed Steve's number in North Hero. It rang and rang. I hung up and dialed Mountain Air, and sure enough, he answered.

"Steve," I said. "It's me."

"Hey, what's up? I thought you were headed to Massachusetts."

"I'm at the hospital. I had a car accident and need a ride home."

"What happened?"

"A lady ran a red light and smashed into my driver's side door. My back is messed up, but nothing's broken. It was her fault. She even admitted it."

"So you're not going to Massachusetts?"

"They took my car away on a flatbed. I have nothing to drive."

"Oh. What do you want me to do?"

He had no interest in helping. "I need a ride from the hospital."

"Can't you take a cab?"

For a long moment, I stayed silent. What a jerk. I could hear Steve discussing a flight with Frank in the background.

"It's just a five-minute drive. Can't you give me a ride back to the airport?"

"What?" He was still conversing with Frank and not listening.

"All I want is a ride to the airport so I can talk to Frank. I'm going to ask for a few days off to get my back straightened out. And if it's not too much trouble, I also need a ride back to my apartment."

"Okay," he sighed.

I sat in the waiting area and cursed myself for not just calling a taxi. Now I looked more miserable than the unhappy people around me.

The chair made my back ache even more, so I stood to watch for Steve's ugly green Pacer from the window. The airport was only five minutes away, ten at the most, but he didn't arrive until forty-five minutes later. He pulled up to the entrance behind an empty ambulance, and I waited to see if he would come in. He didn't. Instead, he sat at the wheel of the car, took a brief look around, and then buried his face in yellow newsprint pages that could only be *Trade-A-Plane*. I meandered out to the car and slid into the front seat without a word.

He looked up. "How're you doing?"

"Not great," I answered without looking at him. "It's been a hell of a day. My car is probably totaled, and I feel like crap."

"Was it your fault?" he asked as we pulled out.

"No, I told you. The other car ran a red light."

"Oh. So where do you need to go? I have to get back to Mountain Air to finish what I was working on."

I released a loud sigh. "Just take me to my apartment. I'll call Frank from there."

We drove the rest of the way in silence. At the apartment entrance, he leaned over to give me a quick kiss. "Take it easy."

"Yeah. See ya." I didn't look back on my way in, just eager to get through the door. At the mailbox inside, I stopped to empty it and stuffed the envelopes under my arm. With the other hand, I let myself into the basement apartment I had been calling home these past months, so glad to be alone.

I sunk into the only chair, let out a deep breath, and glanced through the mail. There was an envelope from Tufts University in the stack. Not sure what news I hoped it would contain, I carefully opened it. "Dear Ms. Ruggiero: We are pleased to inform you…"

Oh no. I was not ready for this. I couldn't even feel happy about it. Not today, not this week. But they wanted my answer within a month. It could wait a month. In a month, maybe I would know.

I folded the letter and put it back in the envelope. The rest were bills. Those could wait, too.

I picked up the phone to call Frank to tell him I needed a few days off to recover from my aches and bruises. He easily agreed and told me to rest well. I then called Dick to pour out the day's events to someone who had no choice but to listen: the accident, Steve, the acceptance letter. He prescribed a refill for the tranquilizer he had prescribed and called it in to a local pharmacy within walking distance.

—

Three days later, my back still hurt as I drove to the chiropractor's office in the rental car I would be driving for a while. When I returned home, the mailman was filling the boxes and handed me one letter, this one from the Summer Language School at Middlebury. It was the second link in my hypothetical transition from aviation.

The news was good, too good. They granted acceptance along with the highest merit scholarship offered by the school. My head spun with the decision I had to make, and I took a tranquilizer and lay down on the bed, the letter still in my hand. *There's still time to figure it out*, I told myself over and over until finally falling asleep.

CHAPTER 32

Final Decision

Flying in late winter can be uninspiring, and this flight was just that. Burlington to Binghamton, New York and back again with a pile of boxes from IBM stashed in the back of a Navajo. I dragged my gear from the airplane when I got back to Burlington and dropped in a seat in the pilot's office. The days were getting longer now that March had passed, but the skies remained gray and thick.

"How'd it go?" Lyle asked me from the doorway. Mountain Air was otherwise quiet.

I smiled. "Okay. Same flight to the same airport. It doesn't change, not even the weather."

"No kidding, but even Binghamton won't be so bad when the sun is shining again. It's been a long winter."

He nodded, his hair in his eyes as always, and continued down the hall. I picked up the phone while completing my paperwork and dialed Steve's number.

"Hi, I just landed," I said.

"Yeah? What's going on at the office?"

"Nothing, pretty quiet."

"Oh."

"Do you want to come over tonight?" I asked.

"No," he responded tersely.

"Well, do you want me to head your way?" I was on shakier ground with each word.

"I don't think so. Listen, Beth, we have to talk about something next time I see you."

"What do you mean?"

"Just that. We have to talk."

"Okay." I leaned forward in my chair. "About what?"

"Now's not the time. Not over the phone."

My heart began to race. "You can't do that, Steve. You can't just tell me you need to talk next time we see each other and then hang up." My voice cracked.

"Fine, have it your way," he said stoically. "I don't want to go out with you anymore. I don't love you."

He made his statement, and with it, he might as well have punched me in the stomach.

"Are you still there?" he asked.

"Yeah."

"It's not that I don't care about you."

"Is there someone else," I asked in a shaky voice. For Steve, the answer could only be no. His whole life was flying, and there had barely been room for me.

"No, there isn't someone else." He was becoming annoyed and bored with the conversation.

"I have to go," I muttered.

"Well," he said, "have a nice life." The words were his way of slamming the door to our relationship shut. He ended the conversation and hung up.

I stared at the wall.

Lyle walked in. "You getting ready to go home, Beth?"

"Yeah…" My voice trailed off.

"Is everything okay?" He walked all the way into the tiny room so he could see my face. I was still staring at the wall. "Did something happen?"

"Yes." I nodded slowly. My eyes moved to meet his. "Steve just dumped me."

"Oh, Jesus. Just now—over the phone?"

"Yes."

"That asshole."

"He didn't want to tell me over the phone, but I made him. He said he had to talk about something next time he saw me, and that didn't sound like it would be anytime soon. So he told me. Just like that. On the phone." I started crying. "I can't handle this. I've become so dependent on him." My body shook, and Lyle put his arms around me.

"Yes, you can, Beth," he whispered, "yes, you can."

I shook my head, and the tears flowed.

"You'll be better off without him."

I pulled back from his embrace and felt an urgent need to leave the airport. "I've got to go, Lyle. Thanks for listening, but I've just got to be alone."

He frowned. "Will you be okay?"

"Yeah," I answered hurriedly, desperate to get outside.

"Call me if you need to talk. Actually, I'll call you later to check on you."

I took my bag and coat and ran out to the car, still the same rental. The drive home was a blur, but when I arrived, I had a liter bottle of Canadian whiskey in a skinny paper bag tucked under my arm. Once inside, I threw my things on the floor and began the long night ahead.

The only sounds in the apartment were not of crying—I couldn't squeeze out any more tears—just my panicked voice declaring again and again I could not move on without him.

The whiskey bottle was open. One third into it, I added a pill. One of the tranquilizers Dick had prescribed. The label specifically instructed me not to combine it with alcohol. So I did.

———

That was the last I saw of myself that night. Except for once, a few hours later. A separation occurred—me from myself. As wretched as I felt the moment before, I was relieved in the next moment as my mind escaped from my physical self. As if in spirit, I floated to the ceiling above and stared down at my pitifully contracted form, heaped over the toilet filled with vomit. As if the poison that had built up after two years with Steve was being violently purged from my insides, the figure leaning over the toilet wretched in uneven timing. It was a sorry thing to watch myself, powerless to help my ailing body. I saw it all in quiet sadness from the corner of the ceiling where I hovered, weightless in form, sober in spirit, and temporarily relieved of the suffering my body was going through down there on the cold bathroom floor.

———

I awoke slowly, the sights and sounds of the room taking minutes to filter through my clouded head. The surroundings were unfamiliar. I closed my eyes again, grateful for the quick retreat. What bed was I in? Where was I? The questions swam distortedly in my head, and I dozed off again.

"She was awake a minute ago," a male voice said between the questions in my head. "It looks like she's fallen back asleep now."

A woman's voice responded. "That's what she really needs, lots of rest. She didn't take enough pills to cause any real danger."

I allowed my eyes to open slightly and recognized Lyle nodding his head in response to the woman's words. He looked down at me.

"Beth, are you awake?" he asked.

I looked to his left and saw that the woman beside him was a nurse. She stood at the foot of the bed.

She smiled gently. "How do you feel?"

My eyes opened a little wider as they adjusted to the light.

"Terrible," I responded. "Where am I?"

"You're in the hospital, dear. The psychiatric ward."

The psychiatric ward? I tried to reconstruct the events that brought me here. Between huge gaps, the last thing I could remember was floating over myself in the bathroom, watching myself be sick at the toilet. And then it came back to me, the strongest recollection, of Steve. I had a sharp pang and groaned.

"How did I get here?" I asked Lyle.

"Paul and I brought you last night."

"There's rarely an empty bed in this ward," the nurse informed me. "But Dr. Schlegel made sure you were admitted."

Dr. Schlegel? Dick. "How did you know about him?" I asked. How far had my secret gone? I panicked, but then seeing my predicament, it was clear it made no difference anymore.

"We got his name from the bottle of pills in your apartment," Lyle said.

"Please don't tell anyone about it, Lyle," I pleaded. "It could end my path to the airlines."

He put his hand on my shoulder and said, "Don't worry, Beth. It's our secret."

Please leave now, I thought to myself, *I need to figure everything out.*

"Get more sleep, dear," the nurse suggested.

She and Lyle left the room.

———

Several more times throughout the day, I awoke groggily only to remember more details, and my eyes quickly closed again. After a long sleep, I awoke in the darkness of night. A sliver of light shining from outside illuminated the clock on the wall. It was three forty-five in the morning. I assumed it was my second night in this bed.

My mind was clearer now, and I had enough strength to face what had happened. For the next few hours until the sun rose, I reviewed everything from the beginning to what I could now start calling the end.

At intervals, I cried, and the pain seemed unstoppable. But then the burden lightened, and a small glimmer of hope for better times reached my bedside.

For starters, the psychiatric ward would not do. I was ashamed for ending up here. I did not belong here, and even if it had seemed so to the people around me, there was no way in hell I would stay.

When breakfast carts began rattling in the hallway at around seven o'clock, I had already showered and gathered my belongings. At seven fifteen, I walked out of the room and quietly explained to the nurse on duty that I was checking out.

CHAPTER 33

Reflections

I woke up the next morning in my own bed. It was hard to tell what time it was from my basement apartment, and the clock was buried under a pile of dirty clothes on the floor. I reached for my watch—six twenty—and rolled over and closed my eyes, dozing off.

By seven o'clock, I was awake again, and my mind was running. Over and over, I replayed the events of the past two days. Then I thought about the past year, two years, and all the way to my first flying lessons with Steve. Things that should have been so obvious to me a long time ago became clear. *How did I let this go on for so long? Was I stupid, or just blind?* I tried to figure out exactly when this diseased relationship had turned bad. Or was it always bad? The questions didn't need answers. It didn't matter, because for the first time in three years I could see how wrong it had become and the damage it did, on my soul, my heart, my mind.

I spent a couple more hours in bed, in deep, clear-minded thought. When I emerged, it was almost ten o'clock, and after a warm shower, I felt cleansed both physically and mentally. My little home begged attention, so I began cleaning and straightening up. Every so often, I stopped to look around and appreciate my surroundings, however humble they were. Proceeding slowly and mindfully, I spent the rest of the morning on this exercise, and it was mid-afternoon by the time I was done. So I lay down on the futon and fell into a peaceful sleep.

CHAPTER 34

Released

The sun cast a yellow glow over the green hillsides of Vermont as it began its dependable rise in the morning sky. The fuzzy outline glowed red off my left wingtip, and the snow patches dotting the mountains glistened, reflecting bits of light. As I looked east from Lake Champlain below, I could make out the familiar Route Seven, the road between Burlington and Middlebury. Soon, the town of Middlebury showed itself, and I smiled with an inner self-satisfaction. The emotion was new to me, and it was good and right.

Only two weeks had gone by since Steve had rung the death knell on our relationship, if it could even have been called a relationship. Actually, it was more of a sickly attachment on my part. As for Steve, I imagined I had become a ball and chain, something he needed to shed. And after he severed the attachment, it was shockingly liberating, even cathartic. In fact, I appreciated he had done the best thing for me, something I wasn't able to bring myself to do. It didn't hurt anymore when we ran into each other at the airport. I had even stopped taking the drugs Dick had prescribed and stopped seeing him. I was no longer in a dark tunnel looking for light. The sun had come out.

My goal and desire to fly for a major airline once again took front and center stage. I fully recommitted myself by turning down the acceptances from Middlebury and Tufts. I had given it a lot of thought, and even though they were coveted opportunities, I couldn't turn my back on the years and effort I'd put into aviation.

Lake George lay just a few miles ahead, and I pulled back the Navajo's power for a comfortable descent to just above water level. The sun continued to rise almost in sync with my slow descent. As I reached five hundred feet, it cast a long westward gaze across the lake, and the cold water sparkled. The evidence of winter was gradually melting away. With the abundance of evergreen trees around the shore, the sense of spring began early in the season.

My hands were smooth on the controls, and the turns coordinated. The assurance I had striven for these past years through Steve now fell easily into place. No longer was the airplane flying me. The door that had been only slightly ajar was now wide open. I finally understood what I'd been missing all along was not skill but confidence.

With the power reduced, the Navajo glided along just one hundred feet above the surface of the water, and I looked down at the treetops and summer cottages along the shore. The radios in the airplane were quiet; I was alone in this piece of sky. Swallowing my last sip of coffee, I threw the empty cup on the floor in front of the passenger seat and turned my attention to outside. Abeam the seaplane base on the lake's west shore, I made a final power reduction and descended further. At ten feet above the water, I pushed the throttles forward and zipped along, the plane's shadow stretching long across the surface of the water.

The plane sped around the tiny islands and rounded the inlets. Just before the last island in the lake, the largest one, I eased in the power for a climb, flying close to the island's treetops and up from there.

The sun fully up now, the runway at Albany appeared ahead, and I prepared to land. Flaps down. Gear down. Speed established. The routine felt comfortable, with no hesitation.

CHAPTER 35

Moving On

"Hey, how're you doing?" a familiar voice called from across the ramp.

I was on the tarmac pre-flighting the Aztec for the evening flight to Montreal. It was dusk, and though I didn't recognize him from where I was, Steve's unmistakable lope made it plain it was him. There had been few words exchanged during the few weeks since we split up, and definitely none of significance.

What could he possibly want, I wondered. "Okay," I said as I continued the preflight without looking at him.

He crouched under the wing where I was testing the fuel, just two feet away from me. I still didn't look at him. "I've been wanting to talk to you," he began.

We moved out from under the wing, and I leaned against the airplane. Standing in front of me, those eyes that had always shown so much apathy now filled with what possibly looked like sincerity. I waited for him to say what he wanted so I could get on with my flight.

"I know you have to get going to Montreal," he continued, "so I'll get to the point. I made a mistake. You were the best thing in my life, and I've regretted what I did. Is there any way you'd be willing to get back together?"

He was actually pleading. If the plane had not been supporting my weight, I probably would have fallen on the ground in shock. Not happy shock, just shock. I gathered myself, though, reeled in the part of me that at one time would have stepped right into his lure, again and looked straight at him. How could he not see what was so clear to me?

"I'm happy now, Steve. For the first time in a very long time," I answered. "I'm smiling. Haven't you noticed? My head doesn't hurt anymore, and I'm flying the airplane with confidence. And best of all, I enjoy being alone right now. So, to answer your question—no."

He thought for a few moments, saying nothing. Then he turned back to the hangar. When he was halfway across the ramp, I called after him, "Steve." He turned to look back. "Have a nice life."

CHAPTER 36

The Majors

On a Monday morning in June 1989, I sat at a gate at Boston Logan Airport waiting for my flight to Kansas City. I would be interviewing for a pilot position with one of the majors, Trans World Airlines, the same airline that had taken me from New York to Denver in the summer of 1976. The same airline that prompted my desire to fly.

It had been a little over a year and a few different flying jobs since Steve and I broke up. The time with him felt more and more like ancient history. Six weeks after we broke up, I left Mountain Air for a summer job in the White Mountains of New Hampshire. I would fly a tow plane, not for banners this time, but for gliders. I towed the gliders to a few thousand feet and released them before returning to the small grass airstrip in the central part of the state. In winter, it was a ski resort, but in summer, it was a vacation area, complete with a thriving soaring community and the opportunity to take lessons.

The flying was fun but seasonal, and when the summer was over, I would need to find a new job. So I was shocked in August when I got a phone call from none other than Ren Ouellette. He was starting up a new Part 135 company in Manchester, New Hampshire and wanted me to work for him. It was called

Granite State Airways. Ren was still embroiled in lawsuits since Peter's crash, but that didn't stop him from using the same Cash Air Navajos to set up a new Part 135 charter company for the business of flying freight. He had moved his base of operations to New Hampshire where he could deal with a different regional office of the FAA than the one that had shut down Cash Air. At times, Ren even used an alias—Roscoe LeDoux—and thoroughly enjoyed finding ways to outsmart the Feds. Occasionally, as with Granite State Airways, he succeeded. I worked for Ren again for a few months before moving on to better jobs with better airplanes, and by the summer of 1989, I had built enough flying hours that the airlines would consider me.

The Boeing 727 touched down smoothly in Kansas City and taxied to the gate. The interview with TWA would be a three-day process of physical examinations, psychological testing, and flight tests in their simulators. I was newly licensed with my Airline Transport certificate, and this ultimate step in aviation filled me with pride and excitement, along with a little nervousness.

By the end of July, I received the phone call I'd been waiting for. TransWorld Airlines assigned me to a Boeing 727 training class in St. Louis starting on September 24, 1989. After seven weeks of intense training, I qualified for the Flight Engineer—Turbojet Powered certificate and began my new job as Flight Engineer, or Second Officer, in the cockpit of the 727. I had made it to the majors.

EPILOGUE

After only one year flying for TWA, the multiple sclerosis I'd been given a " probable" diagnosis for in 1984 relapsed with new symptoms of dizziness and weakness. I was treated, and the doctors gave me a definitive MS diagnosis. I could no longer qualify for a Class I FAA Medical Certificate needed to keep my job. My short career with the airlines ended abruptly.

I wrestled with the disease for the next few years, during which my thoughts returned to graduate school. This time, I applied to Harvard University, and in 1995, I was accepted and enrolled in the master's program for Chinese Studies. It was the most gratifying time of my life.

After graduation, I began working as a freelance Chinese to English translator at the suggestion of my advisor at Harvard. There was little work at first, but as foreign business in China grew rapidly, so did the demand. Now, the demand for Chinese translators is far more than the supply, and it's a profitable job.

I have continued to live the life I wanted, albeit a struggle.

———

Rod Gorham eventually retired and sold New England Flyers in 2001 to one of the students at the school. Only a few months later, the events of September 11 and its aftermath put the school out of business.

———

Steve ultimately received an FAA violation in connection with the hazmat flight for Cash Air. But he was innovative and determined and joined the Air Force in 1991 as a pilot. He was in for twenty years and now flies for Delta Air Lines.

———

Drew Petrucci, one of the Cash Air pilots, went on to fly for a charter company in Buffalo, New York. After the FAA shutdown of Cash Air, *Investor's Daily* hired Drew's new employer to take over the flight routes vacated by Cash Air. During the company's first week flying those routes, Drew crashed into a lake and died.

———

Harry Pace's license was suspended by the FAA in the aftermath of the Cash Air shutdown. He moved to Missouri, and when his license was active again, he went back to flying freight.

———

More than a year after Peter Covich crashed into the Dorchester neighborhood, federal investigators issued a final report pointing to pilot error as the major cause of the crash. Though there was little evidence to substantiate it, they made the determination based on his insufficient flight time.

———

Ken Ahern called me during the summer of 1989, two years after Cash Air had shut down. It was the first time we had connected since then. He told me he had left aviation after the crash and was calling to ask my advice about getting back into it and making it to the airlines. At that time, I was interviewing with TWA.

———

A year after leaving Mountain Air, I learned that Frank Dunning and his wife were ferrying an airplane in Vermont when the engine quit. Frank did an emergency landing in a field, and though he suffered no major injuries, Mrs. Dunning sadly did. She did not survive.

———

After leaving Vermont, I lost contact with Paul DuBois. Perhaps he is still flying, or perhaps he is playing the tuba at Symphony Hall.

———

My Chinese professor at Middlebury, Gregory Chiang, passed away in 2000 at only sixty-four years old. An annual award was established in 2002 by his students, friends, and colleagues, the Gregory Kuei-Ke Chiang Award in Chinese Language.

———

Mountain Air never found out what was in those mysterious boxes IBM paid us to fly to and from California.

Made in the USA
Middletown, DE
06 September 2019